G000107963

Stepfamilies

How to build a stable, happy stepfamily

Merrilyn Williams

A LION BOOK

Published by
Lion Publishing plc
Sandy Lane West, Oxford, England
ISBN 0 7459 3383 1
Albatross Books Pty Ltd
PO Box 320, Sutherland, NSW 2232, Australia
ISBN 0 7324 1355 9

First edition 1995
10 9 8 7 6 5 4 3 2 1 0

Acknowledgments
Thanks to the following copyright holders for permission to use extracts.
Every effort has been made to trace copyright holders, and we apologize if
there are any inadvertent omissions or errors in the acknowledgements.
From *What Children Need to Know When Parents Get Divorced* by William L.
Coleman, Bethany House Publishers, Minneapolis, Minnesota, USA © 1983
From *Diamonds are Forever*, by Ian Fleming © Glidrose Productions Ltd
1956. First published by Jonathan Cape Ltd. Reprinted by permission of
Glidrose Publications Ltd
Professor Ian Goodyer, Professor of Child and Adolescent Psychiatry,
Cambridge University
Miss Ceridwen Roberts, Director of Family Policies Studies Centre, quoted
in the *Daily Telegraph*, 17 January 1994
Joseph Rowntree Foundation
From *Man and Superman* by George Bernard Shaw, copyright © The Society
of Authors on behalf of the Bernard Shaw Estate
From *Strike the Original Match* by Charles Swindoll, Multnomah Press, 1980,
Joseph Rowntree Foundation
Dr Guinevere Tufnell, Consultant Child and Adolescent Psychiatrist, Child
and Family Consultation Service

A catalogue record for this book is available
from the British Library

Printed and bound in Great Britain
by Cox & Wyman Ltd, Reading

Contents

Preface

Fragmented families? Or stable stepfamilies?

As a schoolgirl, I loved history. Not the dry dates and wars of my school books, but the vital characters that strode right out of their pages straight into my imagination. People like Henry VIII, for instance. His marriages particularly fascinated me. How, I would ask myself, did he get away with fooling so many of the people so much of the time? Did each of those women who became his Queen really believe that she was *the* one? The one who would captivate Hal's heart for ever? The one who would put an heir on his throne? The one who could ensure that 'good' King Hal, forsaking all other, would remain faithful until death them did part? Of course, I had the benefit of hindsight; the little ditty that runs:

> *Divorced, Beheaded, Died,*
> *Divorced, Beheaded, Survived.*

But surely, I would ask myself, by the time wife number three, the lovely Jane Seymour, had met her untimely end—surely the next hopeful might be left with just the teeniest of doubts about the wisdom of taking that trip up the aisle towards matrimonial bliss?

It would appear not. And nor, it would seem, have large numbers of hopefuls ever since. Little did I know then, that I would one day be one of them—that, having married in my teens and divorced in my thirties on the grounds of my husband's adultery, I would then, after nearly six years as a single parent, embark upon a second marriage.

It was not without a good deal of anguish and fear that I did so. Fear of repeating the mistakes of the past; fear of further hurt and rejection; anguish over my children's happiness and security—the turmoil nearly prevented my going ahead at all.

My husband-to-be, a bachelor of thirty-five, shared some of my reservations and was (painfully) on the receiving end of others. Looking back, he wonders sometimes how we arrived at our current level of stability. More often than not in those early days, it was simply a case of gritting our teeth and getting on with it, held by our sense of commitment to one another, to making the thing work.

But in this era of instantaneous and disposable commodities (I heard recently of a pop star who never washed his underpants but threw them away daily) is it any wonder that we've lost much of the sense of stoicism and commitment that saw our parents and grandparents through two world wars? Marriage, whether first, second or subsequent, is hard work. But in my experience, so is breaking up. Yet of the 350,000 marriages contracted in Britain in 1991 (more than a third of them remarriages following the divorce of one or both partners) one in every two may be expected to end in divorce. That amounts to a staggering 171,000 per annum, with second (and subsequent) marriages faring the worst.

All too frequently—if newspaper and magazine articles are anything to go by—for many divorced people the idea of finding happiness in a new marriage is an ill-conceived illusion. For them, reality shows 'building a second home' to be a case of stumbling blindly along in the vague hope of avoiding the sort of 'subsidence' that will end up as an ignominious descent into the pitfalls of the previous failed marriage (or marriages). Living in a minefield of damaged emotions that can threaten to blow the entire stepfamily into oblivion the moment any one member puts a foot wrong, the children of such marriages may turn out ultimately to be sad, disabled, dislocated individuals who are almost certainly destined to repeat the formula.

It is in an attempt both to prevent and repair the ravages of unhappiness and despair that lie behind these statistics that I'm embarking upon the writing of this book. Sitting before my computer about to begin, I feel a little like the boy who tried to plug the dams of Holland with his finger. But no matter how small my contribution, I find I can't simply do nothing.

For the fact is that there are no history lessons that concentrate on stepfamilies; no How To classes to attend; and precious few books on the subject. Those I have come across were published, for the most part, in the seventies and eighties. My own attempt (*Second Marriage*) though, I understand, very well received by the majority of booksellers, also raised a good deal of adverse criticism in some quarters before falling victim within weeks of publication to a warehouse arson attack.

I realise that divorce and remarriage are anathema to many, and especially to Christians. But whilst I respect the sincerity of these sentiments, I can't help feeling that there's an ostrich-like element in refusing to read or learn anything on the subject. Burying our heads in the sand doesn't nullify the existence of stepfamilies; nor does it address the issues that they face.

Like it, or not, the fact is that we live in a society where family units are increasingly diverse, with little understanding of what makes for harmony amongst the members of each, and still less on how to handle the conflicts that arise. When it all goes wrong—as it frequently does—then we tend to turn on the church for having 'failed' us—and look to the government for moral and legislative edicts which we fondly, and erroneously, believe will resolve the situation. To my mind, that's about as effective as applying a sticking plaster to a brain tumour.

But that's not to say that nothing can be done. As a Christian, I believe and have experienced in my own life that God works all things together for good for those who love him. It may not feel like it at the time. But that makes it no less true. The Bible says that faith is the hope of things unseen.[1]

When my marriage broke up, after years of happiness all round, I felt a huge sense of relief. Of course I was distressed that it had come to this. Naturally, I felt the pain of severance, guilt, failure and rejection. But the overwhelming feeling was one of release. A certain kind of freedom. Because trying to make the marriage work was no longer my problem. I learned to grow up, to mature and to become the *whole* person that God intended me to be. And then he brought Paul into my life...

In writing this book I make no pretentions to expertise. I'm one of you. And all I can do in the hope of lightening your load, is to share with you some of the principles and insights that have worked for me, my children, and Paul—a stepson himself, long before he became a stepfather to my girls. In addition, there are the experiences of others who have been generous enough to allow us to use their stories.

This book is intended to be a superstore of Do It Yourself relationship-building skills and techniques. Help yourselves to as much or as little as you like. Who knows—you may not only create a home of harmony for yourselves, but actually be an inspiration to others in helping them to build a more stable stepfamily.

Part I

The
Planning Stage

1

Site Inspection

A marriage is a lot like our house. While new it sparkles.
Fresh smells, fun surprises and new discoveries... As time
passes, however... the grit of responsibility mixed with the
grind of routine starts to take its toll... Weeds sprout. Doors
squeak and sag. Windows stick. Paint peels. Roofs leak...
FROM *STRIKE THE ORIGINAL MATCH* BY CHARLES R SWINDOLL.

Those words were written nearly fifteen years ago by
one of America's most popular authors, a father of four,
now adult, children, and a respected Christian leader.
They show a realism about family life that goes beyond
the obvious—to the fundamental truth that any
relationship that requires two people to live together,
intimately and harmoniously for perhaps the best part of
fifty years, or longer; to survive the stresses of modern
society whilst attempting to raise offspring that are half-
way decent human beings; then to come out the other
side as wise and wonderful grandparents whose own
lives are expected to be useful and fulfilling, is going to
be in need of an ongoing 'maintenance scheme': Some
plan or other, that will 'dig out the weeds' of neglected
companionship before they take root properly; that can
'oil the hinges' of dissension; 'smooth down the peeled

paint' of hurt pride; 'release the sticking windows' of entrenched misunderstandings; and 'repair the leaking roof' of damaged emotions.

What's needed, in fact, for our relationships to withstand the rigours of elements and time and still go on looking good and improving, is an understanding of the building techniques that go into making them work. And that is as true of second (and subsequent) marriages as it is of first. Only perhaps more so.

For anyone contemplating a second marriage, the planning stage is crucial. Although it's almost never too late to effect repairs if everything has already gone horribly wrong, there's no doubt that time and care taken at this point can go a long way towards eliminating future disasters. So what is the procedure?

First of all, let's not rush into anything. Whether we're starting out as a stepfamily, or looking to do some maintenance on an existing one, our action deserves careful consideration. Before embarking on any DIY building scheme, we would naturally want to look around and see what expertise is available. What, for example, does the British government see as the answer?

Demolition?

'Then I'll huff, and I'll puff, and I'll blow the house down,'
said the bad wolf to the first little piggy.

If marriage is like a house and running repairs are crucial to the well-being of its occupants, then neglect— for whatever reason—will lead ultimately to a break-down in structure. So, too, will pressure exerted from outside. The sort of pressures we see today.

No one in their right mind would want to condone the breakdown of first marriages or encourage remarriage. However, measures taken to curb the escalating numbers of each must be realistic. Recent attempts to do so in Britain have included the controversial method of exerting financial disincentives on 'absent' fathers. This move, however well intentioned, has proved itself unworkable. The result—the Child Support Agency—has achieved Draconian notoriety.

Whether we believe this to be a genuine endeavour to help bridge the poverty gap in which many single mothers find themselves, and a much needed reminder (like the car-stickers aimed at dog owners) that father-hood is for life—or whether we perceive it, as some newspaper reports would have it, as an exercise in 'lone-mother bashing'—the professed aims of the CSA appear to have failed dismally.

It's hardly surprising. It stands to reason that measures like this are self-perpetuating. Trying to fight poverty of the one party (divorced/single mothers) with swingeing financial obligations on the other (remarried fathers) seems to me to be a lemming-like policy.

Robin Hood may have aimed to achieve parity by robbing the rich to give to the poor, but he worked on the premise that there were 'the rich' to rob. Whilst we can always point to exceptions, the average family *or stepfamily* in the nineteen-nineties rarely comes into that category. One of the post-feminist spin-offs that we're all having to learn to live with has been the sad fact that many households can no longer be sustained on just one income. Women who once wanted the option of outside employment, now find that they have no such choice. Work for them has become simply an economic necessity.

In imposing harsh financial penalties on remarried parents, therefore, government bodies may, in the end, only add to the statistics of broken marriages. And, human nature being what it is, to a further increase of third and fourth marriages under pressure—which in turn become the broken families of tomorrow.

Demolition of existing stepfamilies as a deterrent to others is clearly not the answer.

Nor, in a compassionate society, is turning back the clock to an era where parents are forced to stay in unhappy marriages a viable alternative.

So where *is* help to be found?

Propping up?

Whilst the United Nations designated 1994 the International Year of the Family, and the British government promulgated a (soon to misfire) creed of Back to Basics, newspaper headlines gleefully coined puns around the concept of the Cornflake Family and the Variety Pack.

Terms like 'nuclear family', 'family unit', 'single parent family' and 'stepfamily' have been around a long time, of course. However, there seems to be little or no consensus amongst those 'in the know' as to the effect that these twentieth-century liaisons have on those most closely concerned. Nor on how they may best be helped. Confusion reigns.

◗'Divorce causes depression in children as young as six', the professor of child and adolescent psychiatry at Cambridge University is reported as saying in one newspaper.

◼ 'Bad marriage is better than divorce for children,'

concurred another, challenging the previously accepted view that it is better to have a good divorce than a bad marriage.

■ Broken home children 'not doomed to fail' argued a third, quoting a study by the Family Policy Studies Centre, and continued: 'The disruption children experience from their parents' relationship is more likely to influence their behaviour and educational achievement than the family structure in which they find themselves if their parents split.' And, significantly: 'Inadequate and insecure income can be a source of stress and create practical difficulties for both single parents and couples, in caring for the children.

The message—however garbled—seems to be over-whelmingly that harmony in the home is the key to raising happy, healthy and well-balanced children who, in turn, can themselves become the cornerstone of tomorrow's happy family. As if we didn't already know!

Conversion?

What it does not tell us is how to achieve that crucial state of harmony. And that's where the principles of this book come in. For if Charles Swindoll likens a marriage (or a family) to a house, then second marriages (or stepfamilies) can be likened to a conversion job—knocking two dwellings into one. Before embarking upon such a course of action, however, there are several important factors that need to be considered:

■ A 'structural survey' is essential. The structure can only ever be as stable as its foundations. (Flawed foundations give unstable buildings.)

■ Understanding the blueprint is crucial if the finished 'knock through' and 're-building programme' is to be achieved harmoniously.

■ Since the act of 'tearing a building apart' (a broken marriage) and putting it together again (the stepfamily) is potentially damaging, it's essential to:

● clear the site (sort out and find healing for damaged emotions)

● prepare the ground (establish realistic expectations in all areas, amongst all members of the proposed stepfamily)

● and establish firm footings (building up relationships between all concerned).

Stepfamilies, like first families, are in need of a sensitive planning and building schedule. And that's what we're going to look at now.

2

Flaws In The Foundations

Those who talk most about the blessings of marriage and the constancy of its vows are the very people who declare that if the chain were broken and the prisoners left free to choose, the whole social fabric would fly asunder. You cannot have the argument both ways. If the prisoner is happy, why lock him in? If he is not, why pretend that he is?

GEORGE BERNARD SHAW

Hollywood, soap opera, the pulp press and pop culture between them have sold the idea to generations that

love and marriage
go together like a horse and carriage

and that to sustain the ideal 'all you need is love'. So far, so good.

But it's with the concept of 'love' that the refrain loses its credibility. Love—as either a heady, intoxicating condition, or a state of heightened sexual and physical attraction—is clearly a romantic illusion that has failed dozens of its film star and pop-singer proponents.

Misreading the blueprint

The facts are that

■ experiments with 'open marriage' (whereby each partner was free to indulge in extra-marital sexual affairs), the practice of co-habitation, and lone-parenthood have all fallen short of the promise to deliver, in terms of love, happiness and security

■ love, in its true sense, has at least as much to do with the will as with the emotions

■ 'free' love—the cry of the sixties and seventies—is to be found only in the paradox of commitment.

That's because emotions can go up and down with the barometer. Sunshine, a good meal, a job promotion or a pay rise; a new outfit, a compliment, or a phone call from a friend—all may produce a sense of euphoria that can rub off. It may be easy at such times to feel loving—even sexy.

'Minor' conflicts—such as how we're going to meet the mortgage repayments this month—appear just that: too insignificant to be allowed to intrude upon those warm loving feelings. Even major areas of disgruntlement—like why, whenever we reach for the cornflakes, the packet seems only to yield dry dust which, with the addition of milk, instantly turns to wet cement—can bring the semblance of a smile to our faces.

But what happens when the weather is grey? When we're cold, hungry and tired because we've had to work late, the car broke down in the rain, we haven't had time to get to the shops, the family is in anarchy over the prospect of fish fingers yet again, and *nobody* understands? What happens when a junior colleague becomes your superior; the dry cleaners wreck your new suit;

you're told you're looking a bit thin on top, thick in the middle, and slow on your feet? What happens when the bedtime 'headaches' put paid to your love-life; mum's pre-menstrual tension appears to grip the entire household; even the children behave as if we have bad breath or body odour—and the grass looks greener elsewhere?

Well that's where the will comes in. The will to stick to the blueprint for marriage—exactly as the architect designed it. Not in the sense of 'mind-over-matter'. But because it makes sense to turn to an expert.

Christians believe that God is that expert: that it was he who designed marriage from the outset; and therefore that he knows what makes it work. Irrespective of faith or creed, human experience has shown the biblical specification for marriage to be a good basis to work from, and a reliable means of helping couples who run into problems in their relationships.

The architect's design

The Genesis account of the creation of Adam and Eve states that, although the birds and beasts had been formed out of the earth, that method of creation had not produced a suitable companion for Adam, the first human being. A different tactic was called for.

So the first woman to be formed came out of his body, rather than the ground. However, it was not Adam's act of creation (as in the conception of children) that brought her into being, but God's. She was essentially made in the image of God—but she was also bone of Adam's bone, flesh of his flesh.

It was for this reason, says the Bible account, that Adam and prospective marriage partners are called upon to:

■ leave their parents (and their influence), in order to become an independent adult so that they become mature enough to:

■ cleave (adhere or make a commitment) to their marriage partner.

This is what is meant by the blueprint for marriage. It means that married couples are called upon to:

■ acknowledge that sexual attraction and romance on their own just aren't enough

■ love one another at a deeper level than merely an emotional or physical level

■ accept (what every divorcee knows in some measure or other) that marriage truly makes us one flesh with our partner, and that however 'bad' the marriage, divorce tears us in two, and is a painful option

■ determine (by an act of the will rather than allowing the emotions to dictate our behaviour) to work the thing through. This is what is meant by making a commitment to stick together—no matter what

■ understand that commitment is the true nature of love and transcends feelings. This means that when we don't *feel* loving, we can acknowledge our emotional condition (anger, resentment, frustration) but, because of our commitment, be willing to stay with the situation. My experience as a Christian has helped me to put difficult feelings (and the behaviour they generate) into God's hands and allow him to change me.

■ believe that only in commitment can we find security

■ know that the security that comes from that kind of love will give us freedom

■ benefit from the freedom to explore the skills and techniques of learning how to handle conflict—together

■ enjoy the freedom of being able to be ourselves; not having to wear masks or pretend to be some celluloid Hollywood superstar

■ relax in the freedom of knowing that commitment continues long after beauty, youth and intellect are impaired and cease.

This, whatever our belief, is the best blueprint. The one that will ultimately see us through. It may be hard work, but the 'pay-off' is good and positive. Christians also believe that, for those of us who have laboured through first marriages only to have them break us, there is an invitation: 'Come to me, all you who are weary and burdened, and I will give you rest,' says Jesus. 'Take my yoke upon you... for my yoke is easy and my burden is light.'[2] That, surely, has to be good news?

But misreading the small print of our marriage agreement may not be the only mistake we've made.

Misinterpreting the specification

Most marriages don't add two people together. They subtract one from the other.

FROM *DIAMONDS ARE FOREVER*, BY IAN FLEMING

This cynical view of marriage, once considered exclusively a male bastion for bachelorhood, is fast gaining credence amongst post-feminist women—if certain American TV chat shows are to be believed. The inference is that we'd all be better off unmarried; that marriage diminishes our lives in some way; and that when married, we end up becoming less of a person.

Ironically, this view would appear, at first sight, to be endorsed by married couples themselves, in that traditionally they often refer to one another as: 'my other half', or even: 'my better half'. These references are, of course, actually intended as terms of endearment. And, contrary to the cynicism which takes a derogatory view of marriage as a restrictive experience, the implication here is that it is singleness that makes 'half a person'. Traditionalists are, therefore, of the opinion that we all require the addition of a partner to make us 'whole'.

This concept of marriage—as a means of achieving holism, or fulfilling our potential—might be anathema to post-feminist woman and New Man, but it still shows itself to be prevalent in some circles. Certainly in my experience when counselling, it is one of the prime reasons for much despair amongst the never-married, and could even be cited as a possible cause of their singleness (see p28). It may also be responsible for the spate of divorces amongst those wed in the pre-feminist era (if marriage appears to have failed them in their aspirations); and might account for some remarriages (a second chance of finding the 'other half'). Finally, it is perhaps the driving force that impels those who feel they've been 'left on the shelf' to rush into marriage with whoever happens along simply because that's 'all that is left to them'.

All in all, there seems to be a good deal of confusion as to who and what we are when we approach marriage; and to what we believe marriage can 'do' for us, and to us. The fact is that the truth is to be found in all and none of the foregoing ideas.

■ Marriage can, and should be, an enriching 'one-flesh' experience.

■ Of itself, it can 'do' nothing for us.

■ Nor, without our acquiescence, can it detract from our potential.

■ We can only reap that which we have sown—in terms of our concept of marriage, and our self-perception.

Let's have a look at some of these ideas in more detail. First of all, let's be clear that the romantic notions of the philandering heroes who speak of marriage as 'disabling' or an erosion of self-expression are 'romantic' only in fiction and film. Translated into real life, the behaviour spawned by their way of thinking wreaks havoc with other people's emotions.

That's because such people lack the capacity to make a commitment to any one person. *They*, not the married, are the inadequates: the 'half-people' who by their chosen lifestyle have already subtracted from the sum of their persona. It has been said that a 'great lover' is not someone who can satisfy many females once—even a dog can fulfil that criterion—but a man who can satisfy one woman completely and forever. So much for marriage being detrimental to our integrity.

The Genesis account of creation is held by Christians to show quite the reverse. They believe that, from the outset, God considered that it was 'not good for man to be alone'. This statement, however, begs the question: is it 'bad' to be unmarried? Does it infer that those who have no partner are lacking in some way?

This conclusion is obviously unacceptable to those who take the Bible as the basis of their belief. Jesus, they would argue, was the embodiment of all that was 'good'—yet he never married. The apostle Paul, too, wrote in his letter to the Christians in Corinth: 'Now to the unmarried and the widows I say: It is good for them to stay unmarried, as I am.'[3] But lest he be thought a misogamist, he went on: '... if they cannot control themselves, they should marry, for it is better to marry than to burn with passion.'

There are many unmarried people who spring to mind who might, if they dared, admit to 'burning with passion', and personally, (though I have met one or two to whom the term could be applied) I think it's a cop-out to speak of 'a gift of singleness' as some Christians are wont to do.

Sadly, in my experience during six years of single motherhood, this particular cliché is usually pronounced from the safety and comfort of their own marriage by those who know no better. They speak of this 'gift' as if it were something that is extended, universally, to all who are alone; something, moreover, which is to be coveted. To suggest this to the never-married can be cruel, for it implies a lack of gratitude on their part if they then yearn for marriage. To suggest it to those who are abandoned to bring up children alone is more than cruel. It is crass.

Having been in this position myself, I know only too well what it is to long for a partner—not merely for sexual gratification, but for myriad reasons. I have been on the receiving end of well-meaning church people who have told me that 'Jesus should be enough'. And I have suffered the guilt of feeling that my faith in God was under scrutiny and was found to be wanting.

However I know also, from personal experience, that pain, loneliness, insecurity, sexual frustration, and a sense of inadequacy are just as likely to dog the married as the unmarried. It is far more terrible to have to bear all those vicissitudes when lying next to the one person whose intimacy, companionship and understanding should be capable of assuaging them—if only their 'love' were not being withheld, or pledged elsewhere. On their own, therefore, these are not good enough reasons for wanting to be married.

It is a sad fact, however, that no matter how high the rate of divorce, and in spite of a recent decline in the popularity of marriage (current statistics show a fall in the number of weddings taking place in Britain) we have been conditioned to see our ability to attract and keep a mate as the pinnacle of self-expression and success. In doing so, we imply that there is something odd about those who choose not to marry or cohabit. 'The Relationship' has become the badge of self-worth. By it, we assume a status not granted to the single/widowed/divorced.

Is it any wonder then that the unmarried see themselves as deficient in some way? And that if and when the opportunity arises, there is a temptation to rush into marriage as if it's the panacea for all ills? As if, by doing so, we hope to find our 'other half'. Because without that 'other half'—to whom the married refer so frequently—we believe that we're less of a person?

It doesn't have to be so. When Pam first met Chris he was a bachelor in his mid-thirties and, as such, was considered to be socially 'awkward'.

When you're in your teens, people assume that you must have a girlfriend and that marriage will, ultimately, be on the agenda. By the time you get to your late twenties, they take it that that is a foregone conclusion, and are embarrassed when, on asking after your wife, they discover that you don't have one; that you're that anathema to modern society: a single man.

But once in your thirties, things get even worse. Married people take it for granted that you must have a family. They don't ask. They just assume. And you can see from the look on their faces that when they learn the true state of affairs, they're thrown into confusion. In their eyes, you're less of a person.

But Chris was anything but 'less of a person'. When marriage to 'the right girl' appeared to have eluded him and parenthood seemed to be passing him by, he resolved that he would not allow his single status to deter him from living a full and meaningful life. He took out a mortgage and purchased his own house. His mother had already seen to it in his childhood that he never had to suffer the indignity of being unable to fend for himself domestically, so he set to, fulfilling all his natural instincts of creativity and social integration.

What that house and garden did not go through in terms of structural alteration and sprucing would not be worth mentioning! 'Before and after' photographs showed the extent of the transformation. But it was, without doubt, the pictures of the garden that persuaded Pam that Chris was exactly the husband she was looking for.

Only a gentle, home-loving man could have produced such a profusion of flowers and home-grown fruit and vegetables, she thought. It soon became apparent, too, that he had enough outside interests and activities to bring the sense of space, and the richness of variety into their relationship which she knew every marriage needs if it is not to become stale. A member of several clubs: football, tennis, badminton and photo-graphic, Chris was also a member of a local church. Moreover, it was clear from the way in which friends turned to him as their confidant, that he was a good listener. All in all, a 'good catch', thought Pam.

He (as she was glad to discover!) obviously felt likewise about her. Without wishing to sound smug, she had to admit to having single-handedly brought up her three girls, a dog, a cat and a tortoise over a period of several years; run her home as a bed and breakfast business; and held down a part-time job. Though there were problems with one of her daughters that were later to put the stepfamily under severe strain, at the time when Pam and Chris met, the girl was living away from home. In Chris's eyes, Pam had made a good job of being a single parent. What was more, their interests, their faith and philosophies of life, even their personalities, all dovetailed together.

They fell in love because they each found the other mutually attractive. It was an attraction based, first and foremost, on equality and friendship. And it was firmly rooted in the fact that each, as a 'whole' person, enjoyed a healthy self-respect.

As Paul and I used to counsel some of the unmarried men and women who sought our advice regarding their status,

> *Marriage is not about two halves making a whole. You have to be a whole person yourself, to begin with, in order to be attractive to someone else. Nor is it a question of what marriage can 'do' for you. Rather, it's: What do you have to offer to your partner?*

3
_

Clearing Out
The Debris

In the United Kingdom, where monogamy is the law of the land, only divorce or the death of a partner open the door to remarriage and, therefore, to the potential of a stepfamily. The permutations, however, are numerous:

■ Remarriage of widow or widower:
Dawn, mother of two teenage girls, had been a widow for some years before meeting and marrying John, a divorcee.

■ Remarriage of divorced, single parent to unmarried partner:
Isobel, mother of two girls, had suffered an acrimonious divorce prior to meeting Terry, who had never been married.
Max, father and grandfather, married career-woman Cathy when she was in her forties.

■ Remarriage of two divorcees, both with children from previous marriage:
When Bob's wife ran away with Maggie's husband, their mutual distress and support led, eventually, to their own marriage. Whilst both of Maggie's children lived with

them, only two of Bob's three did so—the youngest remaining with his mother.

■ Multiple families: remarriage of divorced parent with a subsequent family:
Frank, father of two girls who had lived with their mother since she left him, was more than happy to raise a second family when he married Lynn, who had previously been single.

■ Multiple marriages/multiple families:
By the age of thirty, Steve's first marriage had ended in divorce (his ex-wife having custody of their two daughters) and his second wife had left him to fend alone with their two small children. Ultimately, after two years of living with Ruth, who had moved in to look after the little ones, their marriage (her first, his third) produced a further two children.

Subsidence

Divorce or bereavement are both traumatic experiences that can be intensely distressing. Mentally and emotion-ally their victims may be left feeling frail and tottering, rather lke the house of a woman I met some years ago.

When her husband had left her, she had decided to set about achieving her dream of moving from suburban London to the rolling landscape of Devon. By the time I came across her, she had scraped together enough money to purchase a dilapidated little house in a small resort on the south coast, on a hillside overlooking an estuary of outstanding beauty.

Sadly, within months her dream was shattered. Cracks began to appear in the walls she had lovingly papered, and deep fissures in the ceilings. Newly glossed windows began to jam and doors to hang at crazy angles. Outside in the freshly dug borders surrounding the house, it soon became clear that there were chronic faults in the substructure.

A structural survey revealed subsidence. In a detailed report the surveyor indicated that underpinning—the removal of decayed and crumbling materials; insertion of new load-bearing girders; and the strengthening of existing ones—was crucial if the whole house was neither to slide down the hillside into the picturesque estuary, or, alternatively, to impact upon itself, folding up like a pack of cards.

That poor woman had to endure years of expense, heartache and upheaval which, with a little timely advice, could have been avoided. Her mental anguish has its parallel in the experience of emotional upheaval suffered by stepfamilies up and down the country, and serves to highlight several points:

■ Death and divorce can cause all sorts of feelings of anger, failure, rejection and guilt that can spread across the fabric of our lives like tiny hairline cracks in a ceiling.

■ If not dealt with, these unhealed emotions may, under renewed pressure (from the second marriage, ex-spouse, access to the children/stepchildren, financial strictures and many other issues) widen into deep fissures.

■ Whole chunks of 'plaster' may fall off, resulting in 'no-go areas': issues and topics that produce such violent emotional responses in our loved ones that we skirt around them and dare not bring them into the open.

■ These rifts in relationships may not easily be mended, and may seriously weaken the structure of the whole stepfamily.

■ They are often only symptomatic of the real problem, which is subsidence of the substructure.

■ Depression, repressed anger and aggression can develop into mental breakdown or self-destructive tendencies that in turn may threaten to bring down other individual members of the stepfamily.

■ The unity of the stepfamily may ultimately be so destroyed as to be virtually beyond help.

Dealing with the damage

If not dealt with prior to remarriage, damaged emotions (like the subsidence in my friend's house) may carry within them the seeds of destruction that can lead to 'concrete cancer'. And as the cracks appear, so do the 'flawed foundations' that destabilise the marriage 'buildings' they support.

'Dealing with it' includes the healing of damaged emotions, which, for Christians, involves seeking the loving help of God. The Bible portrays God as a heavenly father, unfailingly interested in the hurts and problems of those he has created, who longs to be *asked* to be involved. But like all good fathers, he never barges in uninvited—as Val discovered soon after Alan proposed marriage.

The damage of anger, failure, rejection and guilt brought about by the breakdown of Val's first marriage had, she thought, been 'dealt with' during the years following her divorce. Outwardly, at least, she longed for

Alan to ask her to marry him. 'If we were to be married...' he'd say tantalizingly. Only to add hastily: 'But I'm not saying we will...' Val wished he'd jolly well make up his mind!

Then one evening he did just that. But to her horror, far from being filled with joy, she found herself responding instead with every reason under the sun as to why she could not accept his proposal. Her behaviour became increasingly aggressive. She dredged up every criticism she could level against Alan—and threw in a few more besides. Patiently, he hung on.

In mitigation, it has to be said that Val found her attitude as incomprehensible as Alan did. In a fit of fear that she would lose him, she eventually accepted his proposal and agreed that they should be married. But far from making things better, her vitriol became ever more barbed. Until one evening on the telephone, she knew she had to get help.

'This should be the happiest moment of my life,' said Alan, down the line. 'Instead, I feel utterly miserable.'

Val went for counselling. Over a period of weeks she was led to understand what had prompted her unpleasant behaviour. It appeared that in lashing out at Alan, she was venting all the pent-up emotions of her past. She had made him the whipping boy for all those old wounds.

But more than that, her behaviour was also governed by fear. Deep down, there was a battle raging between her conscious mind and her subconscious. Although on one level she longed for marriage to Alan, her innermost being was hell-bent on reminding her of all the worst aspects of her first marriage. From out of an acute sense of self-preservation, she was actually trying to make herself so rude to Alan that—even though she could not bring herself to turn down his proposal—she was hoping that he would no longer want to marry her. In short, she was unconsciously intent upon driving him away.

Once her counsellor had brought her to the point of accepting that Alan was a completely different person to her ex-husband, and that their relationship was founded on an entirely different set of values, they could eventually pray together, asking God to heal Val's emotions.

This would not, the counsellor pointed out, mean that all the i's would be dotted and all the t's would be crossed. 'Wholeness' in this sense is not the same as 'perfection', he said.

What this means is perhaps best illustrated by analogy. Whilst a baby may be a 'whole' person in that it is healthy and free of any sort of deformity that would impair its development, its ability to control its bodily functions and mental faculties are far from perfect! The potential is there in the form of a sound, wholesome genetic blueprint. But only growth, the passing of time, and experience, can produce intellectual maturity, and furnish that child's internal organs with the wherewithal to respond in the manner for which they were designed.

Reverting to the metaphor of building, we can see that in the same way, weeding out the insecurities of the past and mending damaged emotions is only a beginning:

■ It clears the building site so that we are able to start again.

■ It promotes sound building techniques, by means of which we may reach emotional maturity.

■ It provides a firm foundation on which to build a reliable relationship.

Restoration work

Much of this sort of trauma can be avoided if 'underpinning' or 'restoration work' is undertaken prior to setting up a second marriage. To restore means to make whole, and it's our damaged emotions that are in need of being pieced together. Only when we are people of integrity can we hope to hold everything together in its rightful place.

Like the cracked ceiling, however, our cries for help may initially go unnoticed—unrecognized even by ourselves. We all have a tendency at times to indulge in various defence mechanisms that may actually disguise or distort the problem. Is my anger over a stepchild's bedroom that looks as if a bomb has hit it a justifiable reaction, or is it, in fact, more to do with my own feelings of inadequacy or low self-esteem? Might my anger actually have been triggered off, not by the untidy bedroom, but by a telephone conversation I had with my ex-spouse an hour earlier, in which deep-seated hurts were exposed and from which I feel I emerged the worse for wear?

Now I'm not suggesting for one moment that the damage done during years of marital strife can be healed instantly, but it may be helpful to look at the remedies that can prevent that cracked ceiling from coming down, bringing with it all the surrounding lath and plaster, and a whole lot of filth besides. The Christian perspective is particularly relevant in this respect, with its emphasis on new beginnings. In its simplest terms, restoration work from a Christian point of view can be reduced to three steps: removal of dirt and debris; repair of damaged structures; and treatment to prevent recurrence.

■ Fear is the debris left in the aftermath of divorce. Fear confirms our sense of guilt and failure. It needs to be eliminated if we are to become the whole people whom we are intended to be. Christians believe that 'God did not give us a spirit of timidity, but a spirit of power, of love and of self-discipline.'[4]

This fear can be eliminated by love, because 'There is no fear in love. But perfect love drives out fear'[5] And such perfect, unconditional love is to be found at the heart of the Christian message, demonstrated in Jesus' life and death which reconciled people with God. The mistakes and bad choices that inevitably form part of a divorce cannot alter God's love for us as we are, and the knowledge and acceptance of this love can drive out our fear of further hurt and rejection.

■ Forgiveness is the repair of damaged structures. Like many remedies, it is often unpleasant to take, but, what-ever our creed or philosophy on life, is vital in preventing a recurrence of damaged emotions. It is a three-part application, and should be repeated when-ever necessary:

● Forgiving those who have hurt us whether they apologise or not. Like commitment, this is a matter of the will, not the emotions. We have no direct control over our feelings; all we can do, according to Christian belief, is to bring them to God, tell him that we are willing to forgive, and ask him to make our emotions match our sense of commitment in this respect. Then we make a conscious decision to see the thing through—no matter how often we may fail in the process, and no matter how often we are offended against. For the sceptic asking how many times we should forgive one another, Christ has this reply: 'Seventy times seven.'[6]

Implicit in that number is the idea of unlimited acts of forgiveness—for the same person.

● Asking for forgiveness: 'I am sorry,' are said to be the three hardest words in the dictionary. But the Christian faith is not alone in adhering strongly to the belief that asking forgiveness for the grudges we hold against others and the wrongs we have done them is the only effective way to purge our own sense of guilt. This may a private affair between ourselves and God, but it may also be appropriate to seek the forgiveness of the person concerned.

● Forgiving ourselves is equally important: to offload the excess baggage of self-destructive guilt; to know new wholeness; to begin again with a fresh start. And this forgiveness is made easier by the belief (or faith) that God forgives us and loves us.

■ This faith in God is a 'treatment' which can prevent the recurrence of guilt and hatred. Christian belief has it that faith is available to everyone; that it is a gift of God; and that even when we turn away from God, it is still available if we genuinely turn back to him for reconciliation.

Faith, according to the Christian, assures us of our forgiveness of ourselves and others when doubts crowd in, and allows us to go on forgiving 'seventy times seven'.

Faith affirms God's love for us, says the Christian, when we feel unloved and unlovable; gives us a spirit of power, of love for others, and of self-discipline. Faith gives us the assurance of being 'somebody' in God's eyes, even when we feel like 'nobody' in the eyes of the world.

In my experience, though it's perfectly possible for this sort of restoration work in a person's heart to take place in the privacy of their own home, counselling of some sort is advisable. Friends, however well-meaning, may lack the necessary skill, and may actually do more harm than good. However, a priest or minister may be able to help, or point the way to an accredited counsellor.

Remember I said earlier that a building can only be as good as its foundations? Well, flaws in the foundations of marriage, and cracks in the ceilings of the emotions can only produce a rickety relationship. And who wants to risk *that* at the outset of a second marriage and stepfamily? As Jesus once pointed out in a story he told:

> *A foolish man built his house on sand. The rain came down, the streams rose, and the winds blew and beat against that house, and it fell with a great crash.* [7]
>
> *A wise man built his house on the rock. The rain came down, the streams rose, and the winds blew and beat against that house; yet it did not fall, because it had its foundation on the rock.* [8]

Choosing the right materials

One of the factors architects and builders have to consider is the way in which different building materials behave, and the manner in which they respond to various stimuli. Stresses and bearing loads, environment and atmospherics, extremes of light and temperature and exposure to traffic, wear and tear, all play their part in determining the role and suitability of any given component. Put that component in conjunction with another of a different sort, however, and understanding the properties of each becomes even more imperative.

For instance, expansion strips have to be inserted periodically when laying terrazzo flooring if the whole thing is not to break up. The plasticity of those strips allows individual chippings and mosaics (made of different stones and composites) space to expand and contract without creating conflict with others. Let's have a brief look at the characteristics of different personalities, and see how they behave on their own, and in relation to others.

Incompatibility is often cited as the reason for the breakdown of a marriage, but what does it actually imply, and can it be avoided? The Oxford Dictionary definition of the word 'compatibility' puts it as: 'the ability to coexist; well-suited; mutually tolerant'; but what does that mean in terms of looking for a partner for life? More to the point, how can I be sure that I've really found someone of like mind, and am not simply being swept off my feet in the euphoria of 'being in love'—or the relief of having at last found someone to help share the burden of raising my family?

There are, in fact, several factors to look for, both in yourself and in your intended partner, which can be discussed in terms of a system of classification called the Myers-Briggs Personality Indicator.

■   We need to establish where each of us likes to re-charge our batteries.

● Is the company of others essential to our sense of well-being? Are we extrovert?

● Alternatively, do we find other people draining, and know that we need large chunks of life to be spent in quiet, perhaps solitary, pursuits? Are we introvert?

If each of us is different in this respect, is that to our mutual benefit? Will my partner 'balance' my personality, and I his/hers? Or do these differences in temperament carry with them the bones of dissension?

■ Which method does each of us naturally employ in acquiring and conveying information?

● Is it through our sensory perceptions? Do we lean to detail, facts and figures?

● Or do we find ourselves using an intuitive approach, looking at the broader picture to discover the meanings and possibilities of a situation? Do we favour imagination and inspiration?

If we're opposites in this respect, are we able to understand one another? And to make ourselves understood? Or does each of us secretly harbour negative thoughts about the other's method of communicating? Does the sensor find the intuitive's train of thought flighty and illogical and therefore virtually impossible to follow? Does the intuitive find the sensor's attention to detail nit-picking, pedantic and frustrating?

If we're both the same type, is that going to cause problems: may we either lead very dull lives with no flights of fancy; or, alternatively, be flexible and spontaneous to the point of being totally disordered?

■ How about the realms of decision-making?

● Do we tend towards logic?

● Or are we inclined to allow our hearts to rule our heads?

If we're similar in either respect, will we be in danger of being cold-blooded and calculating in our dealings with the things that affect other people; or shall we find ourselves wallowing about in a quagmire of emotion?

If we find one side of the partnership leaning towards analytically oriented decisions, and the other towards people/feeling values, will we each allow the other to 'balance' our predilection?

■ And finally, what sort of lifestyle do we favour?

● One that's flexible, spontaneous, open to suggestion and perhaps a little untidy at the edges?

● Or something more structured and orderly, with dates planned in our diaries and meals on time, perhaps sometimes a little rigid?

If we're different types, might this be a cause of conflict, the spontaneous partner being seen as hopelessly impractical and the structured one as obstinately inflexible?

Or, if we're the same, could this lead to either infinite postponement of important decisions, or a fossilised lifestyle into which new ideas are never allowed to intrude?

It may be wise when you are considering your personality types to enlist the support of a trusted mentor, someone whose opinion can be reasonably impartial (not a close friend or relative) yet someone who has the interest of both at heart.

In addition to 'character analysis' it's only sensible to establish—preferably prior to making any sort of commitment, if disillusion is not to set in—whether our individual attitudes to various 'controversial' issues are likely to cause problems in the future. Broadly, these can be broken down into four main groups:

■ Sexuality
Can the sexual appetites and inhibitions of each partner coexist in harmony? Euphoria in the early days of courtship and marriage may mask all manner of potentially explosive revelations: questions of AIDS and other sexually transmitted diseases; impotence; hysterectomy; the desire (and ability) to have children;

the existence of children born to us outside wedlock; offspring who have been adopted; abortion: theory and practice. One or other partner may be harbouring a deep-seated sense of guilt (or resentment) in these respects.

■ Material possessions

Do we each have the same perspective on money—the gaining and spending of it? If maintenance is an issue, or the need for a second income, this should be disclosed prior to making any commitment (see also Chapter 6). What about our attitudes to possessions? Are we acquisitive? Or do we hold things lightly? (We may think we admire this quality in a partner—until they start misusing and abusing treasured items.) Alternatively, do we each see ourselves as custodians of the things we possess, and believe that they should therefore be cherished—but not obsessively?

■ Aspirations

Will our personal and family aspirations be mutually beneficial? Are we excited by the hopes and dreams of our partner, while feeling that our own opinions and potential may be fully expressed and realized? Do we both practise the art of encouragement? Is self-discipline, and that meted out to the children, going to create the right environment for our family to blossom? Or does dissension threaten to take over? Do we have a strong sense of family ties within the extended family? With friends? Will this impose burdens on either one of us?

■ Values

Are the world-views of each partner violently opposed? Whilst neither partner should be measuring spiritual 'performance' against the other, nor judging the depth of the other's faith, it would be foolish to underestimate how divisive 'mixed' marriages can be. To someone with no religious belief, the sudden revelation by a partner of a previously hidden faith (Christian, Jewish, Muslim or any other) can be almost as devastating as an act of infidelity. Equally, doctrinal differences within a particular religion cannot be lightly swept under the carpet.

It must be obvious that I've barely skimmed the surface, and common sense tells us that it would be impossible to include every topic within the covers of a book like this, just as it would be for us to evaluate every facet of any relationship. There will always be surprises—and I thank God for that. Getting to know someone within the security of marriage is intended to be a vibrant and ongoing delight. Those who have been married for years may say that they know their spouse through and through, but how boring that would be if it were true.

Nonetheless, there are some surprises that we'd be better off without. Never let it be said that we didn't know this or that about the person we have chosen to marry—simply because we didn't dare ask. Fear of hearing something we'd rather not know is a pretty self-destructive reason for not finding out until it's too late. The old axiom: 'Marry in haste; repent at leisure' has been rendered in modern times, 'Marry in haste, and repent at Reno'—Reno being the American city famous for the quick-fix divorce.

Rather, in a marriage as in any long-term project,

When we build let us think that we build forever.

FROM *THE SEVEN LAMPS OF ARCHITECTURE* BY JOHN RUSKIN

4

Laying Firm Footings

The decision to remarry has been made. It only remains for the children to be informed. But before rushing into an ecstatic declaration, let's be a little sensitive to their feelings.

Digging deep

How easy it is, in the euphoria of having found someone new with whom to share our life, to believe that this automatically ensures that the offspring on both sides will welcome the change as much as we do. We may even be convinced—perhaps with some justification—that it is to their benefit. But unless we take time to listen, to be honest about their reactions and open to their deeper feelings, we may unwittingly be storing up trouble for the future. The same sort of healing that was applied to our own damaged emotions now needs to be applied to theirs.

> *Children do not cause divorces. Adults cause them. Children often feel sad, hurt and confused when their parents separate. However, the divorce is not the child's fault. Children should not blame themselves for it.*
>
> From *What Children Need to Know When Parents Get Divorced* by William L Coleman

It has been estimated that by the end of the century 2.5 million children in the UK will be growing up in stepfamilies. The majority will have been the innocent victims of their parents' divorce, rather than having lost a parent through death. Dr Guinevere Tufnell, a consultant psychiatrist, is reported as having said that:

> *The effects of divorce on children are absolutely immense and we have not been counting the cost of this.*

And according to a study by the Joseph Rowntree Foundation (the first to concentrate on the effects of divorce on children):

> *Children from families torn apart by divorce are more likely to suffer illness and problems at school than youngsters whose parents stay together… And… youngsters living… with stepfamilies reported more difficulties than those living with both natural parents.**

Such studies make depressing reading—especially for those parents who have already embarked upon a second marriage. But for them, and for those contemplating the idea, this need not be the end of the story. We simply need to be aware of the likely problems, and to apply certain principles in the search for solutions if we are to put down firm footings for the future. As the book of Proverbs in the Bible states:

> *By wisdom a house is built, and through understanding it is established.*[9]

---

* The Joseph Rowntree Foundation would like to point out that there are many caveats to the above statement. At the extreme, a marriage that involved physical abuse would almost certainly not be better than divorce.

■ Children need to be encouraged to express their feelings in a non-threatening environment—the privacy of their own home—and in the absence of the prospective step-parent (though as trust is built up, it may actually be helpful to include the prospective step-parent in these discussions, in order to promote the concept of openness and honesty without hostility).

■ Guilts and fears need to be addressed and, where appropriate, gently demolished; for example, the idea, prevalent among many children, that they were in some way to blame for the divorce of their parents.

■ Explanations easily comprehensible to a child should be given as to why the parents split up: a correlation may be drawn with friends at school whose interests take them in different directions.

■ Above all, however acrimonious the divorce, for the sake of the child's future development it behoves the parent who has custody to stress the absent parent's continuing love for the child—but only, obviously, if this is true (a different line may be needed for the child who has been abused).

■ The child needs to be reassured that the remarriage of either parent will not mean an end to that love; nor to access with the absent parent (unless, of course, there is either a Court Order restraining access, or the absent parent chooses to sever all ties).

■ If at all possible, the child needs to be assured of the continuing love and availability of the wider family: grandparents, aunts, uncles, cousins and so on.

Building for the future

In Architecture as in all other Operative Arts, the end must direct the Operation. The end is to build well...

FROM *ELEMENTS OF ARCHITECTURE* BY HENRY WOTTON

One of the chief areas of concern for Alan when he and Val decided to get married was that he might find himself inflicting on his stepchildren the sort of problems he'd encountered as a teenager. He and his father had become exceptionally close after the death of his mother.

But I realized Dad needed a life of his own, and I was glad for him when he met someone else and got married again.

Unfortunately, things didn't quite work out as Alan had envisaged. Even as an adolescent he was aware, in his stepmother's behaviour, of an unspoken rivalry for his father's attention. However, he was too young and immature to have any idea how to deal with it. It was not in his nature to be competitive, so his answer was to back off. His father's solution was quite the opposite! Ever sensitive to Alan's natural diffidence, he appeared more determined than ever to include him in the trio. Alan's stepmother reacted with blatant displays of jealousy, becoming demanding, like a child. There was only one thing Alan could do.

Dad was naturally a very affectionate man, very tactile. I suppose you could say he was quite exuberant. He was like that with Mum as much as with me, but she didn't seem to be able to cope with his relationship with me. He would have loved us to continue going to football together, but she made that impossible. In the end, I felt I had no alternative but to reject his affection

and to make myself scarce. I'm sure it must have hurt him,
but I just couldn't cope with my stepmother's jealousy.

The result was an uneasy formality between himself, his father and stepmother that lasted throughout their lifetime. But the insights Alan gained through these experiences made him particularly sensitive to the feelings of his prospective stepdaughters—particularly those of the youngest, then only thirteen years of age, and the only one of the three still living at home.

When Val and he were seriously considering the possibility of marriage, he wrote to her:

> *... and there is Hannah to consider. I could marry you tomorrow and we know that we could work at it and be extremely happy and content.*
>
> *However—put yourself in Hannah's place—suddenly having to uproot, not necessarily house-wise, but certainly relationship-wise—and having to live with a relatively strange man. She is an emerging adolescent—that's already revealing itself in her conversation with you, even in front of me. Just imagine that she and I didn't get on. That would break your heart. And probably our relationship... I must get to know Hannah—not just as a friend of her mum.*
>
> *Do you want us to be an instant family, or mother and daughter, and man and wife? What does Hannah want? She can't really be expected to answer that yet, as she doesn't know me sufficiently well, but that question must be answered ultimately, darling... Our situation demands more than the normal responses between two people...*

As a result of Alan's own adolescent experiences and his anxiety for Hannah, he and Val discussed the implications at length. Whilst acknowledging the validity of his concern, it seemed to Val that Hannah was already at a certain disadvantage.

*Growing up in a one-parent family with only intermittent
access from her father meant that Hannah was being
presented with a lopsided, feminine perspective on life. Whilst
nothing could alter the fact of my divorce, nor the unhappy
years that preceded it, I felt that her view of marriage was
one thing that could be changed—hopefully for the better. At
least with Alan as her stepfather, the balance would be
redressed.*

It was Val's ardent hope that being exposed to male
attitudes and influences on a daily basis would help
Hannah's understanding of men in general, and that
that, in turn, would be of positive benefit to her future
relationships with the opposite sex. Val also wanted all
her children to see for themselves that marriage *per se*
was not doomed to failure. She wanted them to realize
that, given:

■ a commitment to the sanctity of one's vows,

■ the strength of character to cope with conflict, overcome
the problems, and work at improved communication skills

marriage could actually contribute something of positive
value to one's life and be a happy and fulfilling experience, especially as Val and Alan shared a faith.

Val was realistic enough to admit, however, that none
of that was going to happen overnight. Nor, just because
it was what she and Alan wanted, would it follow
automatically. They both knew that they would have to
have a strategy. And that it would have to be flexible.
Something that could be adapted to meet any contin-
gency. Val explained:

*For months before our marriage (and for years afterwards!)
we talked of little else. With hindsight, our 'plan'—which was*

no plan at all, but simply an ongoing, daily insight into whatever confronted us—could be summed up as follows:

● *Children need to be allowed time to develop a relationship with the prospective step-parent—at their own level. It's easy to believe that because you have come to know him/her well, and are convinced that he/she is ideal step-parent material, that your child will think likewise.*

● *It needs to be stressed—and followed up with appropriate behaviour as evidence—that the step-parent will not attempt to usurp the absent parent, but will simply provide an additional, but different sort of relationship.*

● *As well as 'family time' children need time alone with their natural parent.*

● *Access to the natural parent should never be 'blocked' or intruded upon by the step-parent.*

● *Knowing where you propose living will greatly affect your child's security. Will it mean a change of towns? Of schools? Of friends?*

In addition to Val's points, I would add the following: children need to know where they stand with pro-spective stepbrothers and sisters.

■ Will the new step-parent's children be moving in with you and them?

■ If not, will they be visiting from time to time?

■ In either case, will that mean that your child has to give up cherished areas of privacy? Shared bedrooms? A division of space and possessions?

■ Alternatively, will your children be expected to uproot and go to live with *them*? Share their bedroom? Attend their school?

We'll be looking in detail in later chapters at how some of these issues can be dealt with effectively.

Settling the dust

Parents tend to think it is a good thing when their bolshie daughter quietens down, stops going seeing friends and locks herself away in her bedroom where they think she is doing her homework. This is probably a complete misunderstanding... because social withdrawal is a classic sign of depression.

DR IAN GOODYER, PROFESSOR OF CHILD AND ADOLESCENT PSYCHIATRY AT CAMBRIDGE UNIVERSITY

As parents, we need to be aware of the stigma that still, despite belief to the contrary, attaches to the children of broken homes and stepfamilies. Children as young as five talk at school about multiple 'dads', 'uncles' or 'mum's boyfriends'. However, this seeming acceptance does not necessarily mean that they don't feel 'different' from children who reside happily with both natural parents together. Feeling different may be passed off with an air of bravado; even, perhaps, manifesting itself as something to be boasted about. But inside, the child may be experiencing deep feelings of insecurity, isolation or inferiority, as in Kate's experience at boarding school:

I felt that we were looked down on by the nuns and staff at school. It was as if we were inferior; second class or something...

In fairness it has to be said that many schools insist on the use of neutral terminology in an attempt to overcome this problem: 'unit' instead of 'family'; 'partner' instead of 'husband' or 'wife'. But the sad fact is that the concept of the 'wicked stepmother' of Snow White's fictional experience, or the unscrupulous, uncaring stepfather of Dickensian character, lives on—if not in reality, then certainly in people's minds.

It doesn't take much for a young person to pick up on the fact that successive governments and the media blame many of society's ills on divorced and remarried parents—and therefore, by association, on their offspring. It's well chronicled that, generally speaking, Social Services perceive stepfamilies (along with single parent families) as synonymous with 'problem families', and the children thereof as having a tendency to be 'at risk'.

Is it any wonder, therefore, that whether we like it or not, our children are going to have to face some form of prejudice, however subtle? We need to prepare them for this eventuality—without planting fear, self-pity or anti-establishment prejudice in their own hearts.

Perhaps the best line to take is to present the scenario of playground persecution as being due to ignorance rather than malice. 'It's their problem, not yours,' is one way of putting that across. If, in addition, our children can be helped to see that ignorance is to be pitied, in much the same way that one would pity someone who is sick, then a good deal of the hurtful quality of prejudice may be defused.

However, if this type of support at home fails to meet the child's needs, then other means must be found. Enlisting the school's support, then meeting with the bullies and talking through their motives and the effect that their actions have on their victims—all in a non-judgmental atmosphere of calm—appears to have met with success in some schools, and this may be worth taking up with the headteacher.

Alternatively, older children might be encouraged to champion their cause via essays, debating societies, or through the pages of the school magazine. But whatever action is taken, the aim of the parent should always be to arrest the vicious circle of prejudice-bullying-loss of self-esteem, whilst showing the utmost sympathy and support to the victims, and to promote understanding on both sides.

Planning the new extension

Sometimes children of the previous relationship may not take at all kindly to the new arrangement. In 1995, in two of Australia's best-known TV 'soap' families, children's antipathy towards the idea of the remarriage of their respective parents (one of whom is supposedly widowed, the other divorced) was being played out. The feelings of the fictional widow's teenaged daughter almost exactly mirrored those of Dawn's real-life experience.

> *My youngest daughter, who was about sixteen at the time, really resented it when I said I was getting married. She was so rude when John came to stay, I used to dread it. I thought I'd lose him because of her.*
>
> *I remember one weekend when I took him a cup of early morning tea—he slept in the spare room—I left the door open as usual, but Amy called something out implying that we were having an affair. I was so embarrassed. And of course, it wasn't true.*

The solution to Dawn's dilemma turned out to be simple. Her parents suggested that Amy move in with them. Some time later after a cooling off period, Amy was able to tell her mother that, since the death of her father, she couldn't bear the idea of her sleeping with another man. Suddenly, Amy's rudeness made sense. Dawn had already been involved with someone who had said he wanted to marry her, but who in fact was simply using her to get custody of his child. Dawn realized that Amy's misgivings had some justification.

> She must have thought: 'Oh no! We don't have to go through all that again!' On top of that, my other daughter was getting married just a month before John and me. Amy must have felt she was losing everything. She's okay now though. She kisses John—and obviously has a love for him.

It took time, but talking cleared the air. And once Amy came to see for herself that John was genuine, everything turned out well.

In extreme cases, children may become highly manipulative and take a perverse pleasure in the power of turning the thumbscrew on their parent's guilt. It is my view that they should never be allowed to get away with feeling that they can dictate the terms of their parent's happiness, but I am aware that some youngsters can make everyone's life a misery until the matter is resolved.

If a 'cooling off period' such as Amy's fails to produce the desired effect, it may be that the intervention of a third party is called for: someone impartial, whom the child likes and trusts; someone with the discernment to see through the obnoxious behaviour to the hurt that often lies behind it.

Not all prospective stepfamilies encounter such difficulties. In many cases—especially where a couple's relationship has continued for some years before remarriage takes place, thus ensuring that stepchildren and step-parent have a chance to get to know and like one another—the idea of having a new 'mum' or 'dad' can be quite appealing. This was the experience of both Frank and Maggie.

From the very beginning the sheer goodness of Lynn impressed my two girls. No hint of jealousy from either of them over her! In fact they found it thrilling that they were going to their dad's wedding.

The kids were over the moon when we told them we were going to be married. But they had had two years to get used to the idea.

The age of the offspring may also be a factor, with young children who understand little of the nuances of adult relationships welcoming the concept of a 'new daddy', as Isobel and her husband-to-be Terry discovered.

It was the children who proposed to him. There had been a couple of years when I was the only one on the scene after their father left, and both girls wanted to be a family again. When Terry came along, they kept asking if he was going to be their new daddy. Every time Claire got a new pair of shoes she kept asking, 'Are these my bridesmaid's shoes?'

Both little girls had had a chance to get to know Terry on their own terms. Whilst their mother was back at college qualifying as a teacher, and they were in the charge of an au pair each day, Terry, who had recently returned from a stint overseas, had a spell of unemployment. He put it to good use: mending bicycles, building rabbit hutches and generally making himself indispensable. Isobel was quietly delighted.

It meant they built up a relationship with Terry which didn't include me. In a way, I was the odd one out.

Isobel's children welcomed Terry into the family as someone they had become fond of—rather than as someone who had intruded upon their mother's affection for them.

Sometimes, however, when either death or divorce has left one or more offspring living with the remaining parent, a special kind of bonding can be formed between parent and child, that supersedes the usual parent-child relationship. The two become close friends. In some instances, a feeling of parity may occur; in others, role-reversal, with the child assuming a pseudo-parental responsibility for the parent.

In such cases it can be devastating to the child to discover someone else on the scene; someone who, in their eyes, may be seen as a rival. Jealously protective of their own relationship with mother or father, they may feel that they have lost not only the parent who died or left home, but the remaining parent also. This second 'rejection' may be felt even more keenly than the first, precisely because of the unique and close relationship that has grown up between parent and child.

Of course, such a rarefied relationship cannot be healthy and should never have been allowed to flourish in the first place. But I know, from first-hand experience, the solace to be found for a bruised ego in the aftermath of divorce, when one of your offspring becomes especially close to you. At such times, it's easy to convince yourself that it is to the child's benefit too.

In reality, nothing could be further from the truth. Almost inevitably such a relationship will, ultimately, leave a teenager's emotional and psychological growth impaired. He or she may feel guilty about any activity that appears to be detrimental to the relationship they have with their parent; this can then result in isolation from friends.

'Only' children are particularly susceptible to this sort of reasoning. Though we, as parents, may boast about how close we are to our offspring, we may actually be contributing to a lonely old age for them—and for us.

> *I was touched when I heard Kate whispering into the telephone to one of her friends that she wouldn't be able to go out any more because she couldn't leave me on my own. But at the same time I was horrified. I realised that I had to make a life of my own—fast. I knew I had to convince her (without letting on that I knew what she was up to) that much as I enjoyed her company, I could get along very well on my own.*

This was the view of one mother. But it takes a special sort of discipline to urge such children to pursue their own interests, knowing that in doing so, we may be condemning ourselves to spending our evenings alone. However, the sacrifice that this demands is no more than their due. It is not our offspring's fault if we've been left high and dry. Nor is it their responsibility to provide us with unlimited companionship.

The greatest freedom we can offer our children is the freedom to be young, to be 'irresponsible', to be carefree. But they need our help to assuage feelings of guilt. They need to know that we have a life of our own. A life that sometimes excludes them. A life that fulfils us. They need, from a position of security, to be gently thrust from the nest in order to make meaningful relationships of their own. But the emphasis must be on the 'gently'. Producing a potential step-parent out of the blue can hardly be any less damaging, in its way, than allowing an unnatural parity and intimacy to develop between parent and offspring.

To sum up, how should children be introduced to the idea of their parent's remarriage? I think above all they need:

■ time to allow them to get used to the idea

■ space to get to know their prospective step-parent in relation to *their* world, rather than simply as 'mummy's boyfriend', or 'daddy's girlfriend'.

■ sensitivity, to encourage them to talk out any hidden fears.

■ and finally, a brisk no-nonsense approach, rather than a negative, 'hole-in-the-wall' attitude. Anything less might suggest either that we are aware that there will be problems for them, but that they will have to 'make the best of a bad job'. And we may be placing a weapon in their hands to be used against us.

Part II

The Building Stage

5

Assembling the Building Blocks

Many of the practical details of converting two families into one stepfamily will, necessarily, be thrashed out prior to the wedding. Based on those discussions, a number of decisions may well be put into operation. Some of them, such as what type of wedding service you hope for, may be dictated by the facilities available.

For instance, as a general rule the policy of the Church of England, whilst offering a blessing after the event, does not allow for a full marriage service to those who have previously been divorced. However, don't let that put you off if you have set your heart on a church wedding—particularly if you are a regular communicant. Individual incumbents may well be prevailed upon to conduct a Solemnisation of Marriage, and it's certainly worth asking around.

It's worth remembering, too, that whether you choose to be married with all the ceremony of a church service or something simpler at the Registry Office, a marriage is rarely a private affair limited to the two people being wed. By its very nature it is a public declaration of intent. But more than that, it is the merger of two families—not only of the immediate members who will make up the stepfamily, but also in the broadest sense.

With this in mind, some brides ask members of their husband's family to attend them as bridesmaids. This is another area where great sensitivity towards the feelings of the offspring of bride and groom is needed. Whilst some couples might feel justified in choosing a lavish celebration of their nuptials, it is possible that their children (or stepchildren) may view the proceedings with a good deal of embarrassment. It may feel to them that they are being asked to flaunt their allegiance to their newly-wed parent. In this case, it would be a kindness to play down the ceremony. And if being 'in attendance' in some official capacity at *one* parent's wedding is going to make a child feel as if he or she is cocking a snook at the *other*, then it may be wiser to drop the idea altogether.

Children, it goes without saying, should never be put in the position of feeling that they're having to 'take sides'—however unintentional that may be on the part of the parent.

Putting up a name plate

On that note, it should be stressed that we should never put our children in the position of feeling that they're being coerced into having to accept the new step-parent as a 'replacement' of their natural parent. What to call Mum's new husband, or Dad's new wife, may raise spectres in a child's mind that seem out of all proportion to an adult. But that's no excuse for us to ride roughshod over their inhibitions.

Feelings in this respect will vary from family to family.

Some youngsters will find it embarrassing even to raise the matter at all. They may go to great lengths to avoid using any form of address. Others may find the idea of using 'Mum' or 'Dad' for someone other than their biological parent highly offensive and disloyal. For such children this may actually reinforce the pain and anguish that they experienced at the death or departure of their natural parent.

On the other hand, there will be some—perhaps, particularly, young children—who welcome the idea of conforming to what they see as the 'norm'. They may actually be longing for the familiarity and security of being able to address the two people with whom they live as 'Mummy and Daddy'. If this is so then, in the best interests of the child, it may be politic to discuss the subject with the absent parent, in order to eliminate any ill-feeling.

Whatever the situation, our part as adults is to provide:

■ a sympathetic listening ear

■ an acceptance of whatever makes the child comfortable

■ and an assurance that no pressure will ever be brought to bear when it comes to forms of address.

Bob and Maggie's children all responded differently:

> *I was always 'Dad' to Maggie's girls, but my eldest son always called Maggie by her Christian name.*

Maggie admitted that she had accepted her stepson's form of address when she'd married his father, because, at the time, he had seemed very grown-up to her compared to her own little girls. Only with hindsight did she realize that he was actually not very big himself. Years later, when his sister wished to follow suit, Maggie found that her thinking had shifted.

> *When Sonia was thirteen and wanted to call me by my Christian name, I objected and wouldn't allow her.*

But gradually it became apparent that Maggie's stepdaughter, though grappling with feelings of disloyalty to her natural mother, actually felt excluded every time she heard Maggie's two girls calling their mother 'Mummy'. Only through the intervention of one of Maggie's friends was the matter ultimately resolved. Maggie realised that her stepdaughter had been sidestepping the issue.

> *She'd never really called me anything. Eventually, a friend asked her what she would really like to call me and she said: 'Mummy'. I think she felt left out being the only one of the three girls not to call me 'Mummy'.*

Isobel's little girls, who, throughout Terry's long courtship of their mother had always addressed him by his Christian name, couldn't wait to call him 'Daddy' when they knew that a wedding was to take place. Permission to do so was granted by their natural father. But even so, initially, they found the switch to 'Daddy' caused them much embarrassment and mirth. Once accomplished, however, it appeared to be the most natural thing in the world. Now adult, neither stepdaughter has encountered any problem in having used the same form of address for both father and stepfather all these years and both 'Daddies' have coped with equanimity.

Steve's children, both very young at the time of their father's remarriage, responded similarly, as Ruth explains:

> *Kevin's wedding present to me was to call me 'Mum'. I started as 'Ruth', then 'Mummy Ruth'. But when we got married he asked what he should call me, and I said: 'Anything you like—as long as it's not nasty.' 'I'll call you Mum then,' he said. And his real mother has been very good about it.*

That's not always the case, of course. Nor is the vexed issue of what to call a step-parent necessarily only the dilemma of the child. There are step-parents *themselves* who are not very enamoured of the thought of being addressed as 'Mum' or 'Dad'—as Alan confided when taking on three teenaged stepdaughters.

> *I was seventeen when my mother died, and nearly twenty when my father remarried. But my brother and I were very definitely expected to call my new stepmother 'Mum'. It never came naturally.*
>
> *Frankly, remembering how awkward I felt, and having been a bachelor for years before marrying and becoming a stepfather, I would have found it very daunting being addressed as 'Dad' by my stepdaughters.*

Twelve years later, still 'Alan' to his stepdaughters (though they refer to him and their mother collectively as their 'parents') he is more than happy to be 'Grandpa' to his four small grandchildren-by-marriage—whilst their real grandfather, whom they see infrequently, is addressed more formally as 'Grandfather'. Since toddlers have no concept of how many grandparents they should have, the children's parents feel that until they start asking questions, this will probably cause them the least confusion.

Choosing the site

Mid pleasures and palaces though we may roam,
Be it ever so humble, there's no place like home.

J.H. PAYNE (1791–1852)

One of the practicalities which may be hardest of all to resolve is in the matter of where to live. Of course, it's not all negative. There may be very good reasons for welcoming a move. Single parenthood brings its own set of problems which, in extreme cases, may include squalid housing; impoverished local schools; an unsavoury environment and undesirable 'friends' for the children. If so, then the idea of trading them for something better will be highly appealing.

Nonetheless, it is unwise to underestimate the impact that a move can have on all concerned. Giving up cherished friendships and familiar surroundings—however bleak—rates high on the scale of stress factors. To begin with, Pam tried to shut her mind to the ramifications:

Because Chris had just bought and gutted his house ready for renovation, initially we lived in mine and he commuted the twenty or so miles to work. We'd made up our minds to sell both our houses and start again together. But although we'd decided that we would have to move to his town to be near his job, deep down, I was hoping that a miracle would happen and he'd find a job in my town so we wouldn't have to move.

His house sold quite quickly, but it took nine months after we were married for mine to sell. We had one or two tiffs about it because I wasn't pushing it. I'm ashamed to say, I dressed up my outward show of complacence in spiritual terms. But eventually, it became clear that we would be moving, and I accepted it. Or so I thought.

In practice, I actually found it much more difficult. For a start, I had to give up my part-time job, several voluntary positions that I enjoyed, and I had to cope with all the upheaval of my daughter moving schools only two years before she was due to start her 'O'-levels. She, poor thing, ended up having to do re-sits because of the disruption of moving house and school, and having to learn to live with the whole new concept of a stepfamily.

Anyway—one day when Chris came home, I broke down. 'Everywhere I go,' I wept, 'I see people relating to each other: housewives with their shopping baskets standing on the pavement chattering together; friends meeting for a coffee in the local cafe; mothers nattering outside the school gates—and I know no one.' It may sound pathetic, but I felt absolutely lost.

Fortunately, Chris was sensitive enough to discern that the real problem for Pam and his stepdaughter was not only the loss of friends, purpose and status, but also the fact that they'd moved to the town in which *he'd* grown up from childhood, and were going to the church in which *he'd* been a member for over twenty years.

What friends I had—and I'd never made any close friends— had known me all my life; and what's more, most of them were single so they didn't really relate to us as a couple. We all—in our different ways—felt misfits.

We'd agreed that Pam wouldn't get another job, and also that we'd give ourselves six months after our move to settle down as a married couple before committing ourselves to any specific activities. But of course, being at home all day, with no niche anywhere, just made Pam feel thoroughly isolated.

Chris and Pam decided to bring things forward, but even then, the solution took a while to take effect. Taking up the threads of some of the activities she'd left behind, Pam gradually settled in, made friends and found her 'niche'. In time, Chris found it less embarrassing to face old friends who had known him as a bachelor. And between them they made a point of asking people round to share a meal, and made a whole new set of married friends.

But although Pam's teenaged daughter established a good relationship with her new stepfather quite quickly in the privacy of home, it was to take considerably longer before she felt comfortable amongst her contemporaries at church and school. In an era when stepfamilies were a rarity in Christian circles, she felt at a disadvantage. Consequently, she found herself relying more and more on her mother and Chris for company.

That sense of inferiority was to dog her for many years; in fact, into adulthood. Only then, when she'd been away to college, and when stepfamilies were more commonplace, did she find she'd gained sufficiently in confidence to feel really at home with her peers.

Dawn found her situation just as difficult. When she and John married, she sold up the home she'd shared for most of her adult life with her first husband (and had continued to live in after his death) and moved into his. It didn't take long before she regretted that decision.

I wish we'd both sold up and bought something together. Even though John bought his house after his divorce—so his first wife never lived there—I felt like a lodger. To me, it's his house; he makes all the decisions, and I don't feel free to change anything.

Having always assured Dawn of her freedom to effect the changes she wanted, John found it difficult to understand her diffidence. But she was the newcomer to the household, whereas John and his children had lived in the house and imposed their identity on it for some years. What was more, John lived twenty miles from the town in which Dawn had grown up. Her move had necessitated her giving up not only her job, but perhaps more importantly, the availability and emotional support of her wider family and friends.

> *I was so lonely and homesick, I had to keep going into town just to get away from the four walls of the house. But I felt just as bad there. Everyone seemed to know someone except me.*

One solution, clearly, would have been for Dawn to find a new job, but John needed her at home to answer the telephone for his business, a role previously undertaken by his mother, who had also cooked and cleaned for the family. Not unnaturally, Dawn was reluctant to risk her mother-in-law coming back and taking over, so to begin with she dared not pursue any alternatives. Eventually, however, a compromise was reached. Dawn's father's firm had a mid-week vacancy which he offered her. And on the days that she went out to her job, John worked from home so that he would be available to answer any telephone queries for himself.

In Dawn's and Pam's situation, Voltaire's observation: 'Work banishes those three great evils, boredom, vice and poverty,' proved the answer. But it doesn't have to be paid employment that paves the way into a new life.

■ Children's clubs and organizations, church based activities, leisure centres and sports' clubs all have the merit of involving the whole family.

■ Voluntary work such as charity shops, meals on wheels, or training to staff the local branch of the Citizen's Advice Bureau or Samaritans, as well as creating opportunities for new friendships, have much to offer in giving a sense of satisfaction and purpose.

■ Evening classes, writers' circles, ramblers' groups and clubs specializing in hobbies, in addition to opening up new ways of meeting people, all have the advantage of broadening our horizons and helping to ease the discomfort of dislocation.

When Steve and Ruth began to live together, it was the stigma of 'living in sin' (*sic*) rather than living in what had been his second wife's house, that upset Ruth.

> *Steve had always said it was my home and I could do what I liked in it. But one night when I couldn't sleep, I came down and put all the pictures and ornaments that had belonged to Yvonne in a box to be put away. Steve came down and found me and asked what I was doing. I said: 'You told me I could,' and he laughed and said: 'Yes, but couldn't it wait till morning?'*

Despite the light-heartedness, Ruth's feelings of never truly being mistress of their home continued even after they were married until, some years later, they bought another house. Only then did she realize the extent of her inhibitions about taking on what had been her predecessor's place. Echoing the sentiment of many women in similar situations, she said:

> *When we moved, I realized it* [the first house] *had never really been a home.*

What are the options?

■ For some couples—particularly in today's economic climate—the choice of where to live may be dictated by the location of the main breadwinner's job.

Larger families may find the size of available accommodation a priority.

■ Although staying in their own home may provide security and stability for the children of the stepfamily, having a step-parent move in with them may create problems of a different sort (see Chapter 9).

Alternatively, a move involving the loss of friends, Saturday job, and sense of place in society/church straight after the remarriage of their parent, may lead to considerable loss of identity/self-esteem—at a particularly vulnerable time.

If the parent also finds a move difficult to cope with for the same reasons, he/she will be less able to provide the emotional stability required by the offspring of the household. If at all possible, it may be better to delay a move until the stepfamily has 'gelled' together.

■ Once it is established who will be moving in with whom, (or jointly purchasing a new house) it's imperative that, as well as taking one another's friends on board, the couple makes every attempt to make new friends together.

In this respect, it's helpful if every effort is made to acquire friends on a family basis—by making barbecues, picnics, outings and parties occasions for all ages.

■ It is advisable never to transfer ownership of your home, and that of your children, into the sole name of your partner.

Where there is any question of such matters, legal advice should be sought.

Whilst these issues in themselves may cause a certain amount of dissension and emotional upheaval, others may have far-reaching repercussions in the future development of the children. In this respect, it may be their needs, rather than any financial or housing concern, that have to take precedence.

■ A change of schools mid-way through the GCSE or 'A'-level curriculum could have disastrous consequences for the child's examination, further education, university, and possibly employment prospects.

A quiet word with the headteacher, alerting them to the fact that the child's move is due to your recent remarriage may be worthwhile.

■ Children who are already emotionally disturbed may find the upheaval of a move, necessitating a new town and new school, the final straw.

In such cases, if at all possible, it may put less strain on the stepfamily for the child to remain at the same school, and for the breadwinner(s) to commute to work until things improve.

■ Where a move means putting considerable distance between the children and natural parent on either side, access may prove an insurmountable problem on the grounds of costly and time-consuming travel, and be the cause of further strain on relationships in the stepfamily.

Flexibility, as always, is paramount. Situations do change—often more rapidly than expected.

For an important last word on property and ownership, see Chapter 6 on wills.

6

Costing the Conversion

Suppose one of you wants to build a tower. Will he not first sit down and estimate the cost to see if he has enough money to complete it? For if he lays the foundation and is not able to finish it, everyone who sees it will ridicule him, saying, 'This fellow began to build and was not able to finish.'[10]

Not for nothing is money (mis)quoted as being the root of all evil. The cynics would have us believe that 'When poverty comes in at the door, love flies out of the window'. And though we might baulk at the idea that money should have such an influence on our emotions, most, if not all of us, at some time or other, would willingly join with writer Katherine Mansfield in saying: 'I must say I hate money, but it's the lack of it I hate most.'

As an economic necessity (in the absence of a system of barter) it is a fact of modern Westernized society that cannot be escaped. But money is more than simply a form of currency and means of exchange. The whole issue of how we perceive its acquisition, possession and disposition has the power to raise passions that beggar belief. It can be said to be a measure of our 'worth'— think of the status attached to wealth, salary and gifts.

Extraordinary feats of courage, sometimes on the part of the sick and disabled, can raise huge sums to help others. At the other extreme, people kill for money. Debt, deceit, fraud, usury, greed, miserliness, blackmail and embezzlement taint human nature, whilst their more positive counterparts, self-sacrifice, generosity and charity, do us credit.

It would be naive to think that financial matters play no part in matrimonial conflict. Almost without exception, when marriages break up they are reduced to the simple component of cash. *How To Apportion Possessions* follows hard on the heels of *How To Apportion Blame*—and, in the end, it all boils down to the question of *Who Pays What To Whom*. Yet whilst sex-manuals to help the soon-to-be-married, newly-married, and (more recently) the over-fifties proliferate, there appears to be precious little in the way of advising couples on how to find a meeting point between their different outlooks on money.

For second marriages, the issues are even more crucial. In addition to the complications of trying to accommodate the practicalities and legal requirements of financing two (or more) families, we may find ourselves faced with the very real difficulty of having to redefine and rethink our attitudes. The patterns of earning, spending, giving and saving, having had their foundations laid in childhood and been built upon in adulthood, may, quite unconsciously, have become set in concrete during a first marriage. To overlook their importance at the core of any discussions on remarriage could prove, in the language of metaphor, to be the equivalent of knocking two houses into one, only to find that the floor levels of each are hopelessly misaligned. Exploring the following issues might save a good deal of 'aggro' in the long run.

Budgeting the building

Annual income twenty pounds, annual expenditure nineteen nineteen six, result happiness. Annual income twenty pounds, annual expenditure twenty pounds ought and six, result misery.

DAVID COPPERFIELD BY CHARLES DICKENS

Budgeting the household accounts is bound to be a particularly sensitive area for those embarking on second marriages. This is especially true of the wife/mother who gave up her independence along with paid employment in exchange for domesticity and child-raising in the first marriage, then 'enjoyed' a spell of autonomy as a single parent. Relinquishing control of the purse-strings once more could prove the biggest instance of trust—or foolhardiness—she is asked to make.

It is, therefore, worth being scrupulously sure that the financial aims and attitudes of both husband and wife are at least compatible. A better option yet may be to incorporate some scheme whereby both partners continue to enjoy a certain amount of independence and parity. The following statements reveal a problem that is commonplace.

Losing my widow's pension when I remarried made me feel I was losing all independence.

When we went away on holiday, I wanted to be able to take some money of my own so I could buy presents for my family without using what I consider is John's.

■ Some couples find joint bank accounts are the answer to the question of independence.

74

Others are not so sure:

> *John gives me the housekeeping, but if I want something extra I can have it. He knows I'm not extravagant. I'm very careful, so he trusts me.* We have got a joint bank account, but I have never written a cheque.

> *Any money that comes in from the business is joint. Eventually, when a surplus has built up in the business account, we take it out and put it to earn interest.* We still have to decide whether to have a joint Building Society account.

> *I would have liked for all our money to be pooled—from the sale of our houses and all we had before we were married. But in some ways, I would like to have something of my own in case something should happen to my girls.* I would like to feel I could get at it quickly in an emergency.

■ Yet others prefer to divide financial responsibility, with each having autonomy in clearly defined areas.

> *We found it more suitable to take responsibility for various aspects of the family budget. For instance, I am responsible for the payment of our mortgage each month, and Max sees to the bills each quarter... and to holidays.*

> *We both had incomes when we married, and we both wanted to keep them separate. That way, we felt we'd know where we were. So we worked out exactly what our expenses would be per month, over the whole year. Then we sorted out who could afford what.*

> *Because we were living in my house, we felt it was important that the children should realise that it was actually their stepfather who was keeping them. So Alan pays everything to do with the house—the heating bills, telephone and so on. He also gives me money for food for the family. But I pay for clothes for us all—and Christmas, birthdays and 'extras' come out of my income too.*

There are advantages and disadvantages to each method. Paul and I favoured separate bank accounts, with each of us being responsible for specific, previously decided, areas of expenditure. This was partly because we married in our late thirties and were both used to 'being our own boss'. And partly because we are both fairly methodical people who like to know exactly where we are with our financial arrangements, and take pride in managing our accounts. Our scheme, like any other, has merits and drawbacks and may not suit everyone.

Advantages:

each can

■ effect economies in specific areas to save for some special item of expenditure,

■ be more lavish in other areas

■ or simply put something away for a 'rainy' day.

Disadvantages:

if one partner is not very reliable about budgeting or paying bills or tends to be forgetful, it might then come as a huge shock to the other partner to discover that vital bills have not been paid.

In such instances,

■ mortgage arrears might accrue (and prove impossible to meet, with the result that the house could be repossessed)

■ household insurance or life assurance may lapse—with dire consequences

■ or essential services like gas, water and electricity may be cut off.

In this case, joint bank accounts may be the better option. Or, if sufficient trust exists between the couple, the partner who is the more reliable may take on the role of budgeting, and paying all bills—regardless of gender, or who earns the source of income.

One way to sort out an equitable budget is as follows:

■ Itemize regular bills, total each, and multiply for annual amount: this example is for a British family of four.

Weekly		£	Multiply	Annual Total
School lunches x 2		10.00		
Fares x 2		8.00		
Milk + newspapers + incidentals		15.00		
	Total	£33.00	£33.00 x 52=	£1,716.00
Monthly				
Rent or mortgage		200.00		
Food x 4		200.00		
Petrol		50.00		
Credit cards		100.00		
	Total	£550.00	£550.00 x 12 =	£6,600.00
Quarterly				
Gas		100.00		
Electricity		60.00		
Water rates + council tax		200.00		
	Total	£360.00	£360.00 x 4=	£1,440.00
Annual—for example, Standing Orders, Direct Debits				
House insurance		300.00		
Car tax and insurance		300.00		
Entertainment		200.00		
Subs for Leisure Centre		120.00		
	Total	£920.00	=	£920.00
Grand Total				**£10,676**

■ Divide annual total by twelve to reach monthly expenses of. For the example, given, £10,676/12 = £889.66—say £890 per month.

■ Deduct this from monthly income—say £950 net (after tax and deductions) to give £60 'surplus'.

■ Set aside—in Building Society or separate account—money for repairs and replacement: for example car, lawn mower, house maintenance.

■ If you're lucky: use what's left over for a holiday!

Variations on this method can include:

■ setting up standing orders through your bank to make ten or twelve equal payments to each of the utilities and services such as council tax, water rate, electricity, gas, telephone. Most have facilities for doing this and will gladly send appropriate forms to be filled in.

■ setting up standing orders to pay directly from your bank account into a building society (or other) account for the essentials listed above—and then living on what remains

■ paying 'housekeeping' (which may include news-papers, entertainment fund, gift fund and clothing) by direct debit straight out of the main breadwinner's account into that of the main 'household manager'—and keeping what remains for regular bills.

■ setting up a regular, either jointly-owned, or individual 'rainy-day' savings scheme.

Maintenance: support for existing structures

Suffer the women whom ye divorce to dwell in some part of the houses wherein ye dwell; according to the room and conveniences of the habitations which ye possess; and make them not uneasy, that ye may reduce them to straits.[11]

If a man sells his daughter as a servant, she is not to go free as menservants do. If she does not please the master who has selected her for himself, he must let her be redeemed. He has no right to sell her to foreigners, because he has broken faith with her. If he selects her for his son, he must grant her the rights of a daughter. If he marries another woman, he must not deprive the first one of her food, clothing and marital rights.[12]

If anyone does not provide for his relatives, and especially for his immediate family, he has denied the faith and is worse than an unbeliever.[13]

Most of the major religions of the world recognize that where divorce is an option, it follows that there has to be a financial obligation for the care of the children and their mother. Likewise, the laws of any civilized society also recognize that need. What changes is the way in which 'need' is interpreted. And the manner in which it may best be met.

In this respect, British (and American) thinking is undergoing radical change. Against a background of 'no-fault' divorce, governments are now concerned with legislation that seeks to curb the growth in single parents and, more specifically, the number who are dependent upon social security benefits. Hence the advent, in Britain, of the Child Support Agency. The situation currently prevailing is a mish-mash of old-style divorce-court settlements and the comparatively newly formed CSA.

There is now an obligation on single parents (usually mothers) to disclose the whereabouts of their children's absent parent (usually fathers) in order that the CSA can:

- assess the extent of the 'absent' parent's ability to maintain the children of the partnership

- decide the amount of their financial obligation

- and apply the necessary measures to ensure payment of that sum.

There are two schools of thought as to whether these measures are intended to be punitive (against unmarried mothers and absent fathers) or whether they are a genuine attempt both to improve the welfare of the children of single parent families, and to place responsibility for the support of the family firmly on the shoulders of parents, rather than on those of the taxpayer. The success of the venture is, therefore, highly subjective, depending upon which group we fall into.

Media attention has tended to focus largely upon sensational stories. These have taken several forms. There are those of mistaken identity—where the CSA has written to certain individuals claiming, quite wrongly as it turned out, that they have fathered children born to women other than their wives. And there are those of misguided zeal, where the professed aims of the CSA—to chase up and secure payment from absent fathers who have reneged on their responsibilities—have been shelved in favour of the easier (and therefore more lucrative) option of 'leaning on' those who are already paying, and increasing their financial burden. Needless to say, this sort of measure puts severe strains on existing stepfamilies. The result, as one man pointed out, appears to benefit no one but the Treasury.

I've been paying maintenance for my little boy for the past eight or nine years. It's gone up gradually, and—yes, I've got into arrears once or twice with the job situation as it is, but I've never stopped paying. Then the CSA reassessed it. My ex-wife and her husband are both collecting social security. She's beside herself thinking that she's going to be fifty quid a week better off from me, but what she doesn't seem to realize is that she's going to lose it in benefit. They'll dock her the same amount.

Anyway—I can't pay any more. After all these years on my own, I remarried last year. All I need now to make me completely happy would be the patter of tiny feet. But my wife and I—we haven't a hope of having a family. Couldn't afford to, even without this increase from the CSA.

As far as lone mothers are concerned, here, too, the outcome is divisive.

There are those who are financially better off under the new system, and who welcome the gain in peace of mind and self-esteem that this has brought them. They see the CSA as a buffer in that they, personally, have been relieved of the necessity of chasing non-payment of maintenance through the courts; the uncertainty that this causes; and the indignity of having to see-saw on and off income support until the matter is resolved. Regular maintenance payments, moreover, often enable them to take a job if they choose, since they are no longer obliged to declare any additional income to the Department of Social Security and see their benefits reduced.

On the other side of the argument are those mothers who prefer a 'clean break' settlement. Many want no contact with ex-partners, fearing that the involvement of the CSA will merely result in harassment from them or, worse still, actual violence.

Meanwhile, the battle rages on and, according to a report made by the National Association of Citizens

Advice Bureaux (NACAB), not without its casualties. It appears that attempts to reform the maintenance system have resulted, so far, in an increase in family conflict, and a greater threat to the emotional well-being of the children concerned.

So much for the government's efforts to apply a certain moral code on the whole issue of whether the State or the parents should be responsible for the financial support of children. NACAB is quite right to identify the impact that this has on the children themselves. The long-term effects are difficult to quantify. But according to a TV programme broadcast in 1995, many parents are no better off than they were prior to the advent of the CSA. Others, like the following mothers and daughters, feel that had the CSA been in existence in their time, it would have made things easier for them.

My ex-husband suddenly stopped paying maintenance for my youngest child, with the result that I had to remove her from boarding school. The trauma of having to move schools, on top of the divorce itself, affected her very badly. Apart from having to cope with losing all her friends and settling in to a whole new environment, it upset all her exam options. The new school had a different Board of Examiners, and therefore different subjects. She didn't have very good passes, and had to take them all again.

I had to go to court because my ex-husband stopped paying maintenance. I was awarded a year's back pay, but the solicitor's fees swallowed all that up, and my ex-husband still didn't pay. When I eventually remarried, my new husband had to feed and clothe my daughter. She found it quite upsetting, knowing that her own father had washed his hands of her.

It was hard knowing that Dad was Dad to his second wife's kids, when he couldn't even be bothered to remember my birthday.

Whatever the system and in whatever form maintenance is payable, it is a matter which needs to be brought out into the open if the second marriage is not to suffer unduly. Understandably, there can be a good deal of resentment on the part of second wives if they feel that they are going to end up having to work simply in order to meet payments to the first wife. They have a right to know what they are letting themselves in for. And even then, the situation demands understanding and sensitivity.

> *We were very poor at one stage. The maintenance came first for me, and though my second wife agreed in principle, the test comes in practice. I'd lost the house—my first wife needed it for the kids. We were all living in the same town, and there was a lot of bad feeling between the two women all round.*

> *I missed the kids dreadfully. There she was [the first wife] living in a great big house, and Yvonne and I were in a grotty council house.*

> *You can't afford to play games. Ruth knew exactly what she was getting into right from the word go.*

Even where a policy of openness has prevailed in the second marriage, the thorny subject of maintenance can be a source of hassle that goes on for years.

'It's always been a red rag to a bull,' Isobel said of her ex-husband's erratic payments.

'It would be nice if we didn't have to bother,' Terry agreed.

There are other forms of 'maintenance' that need to be declared. Sometimes it's an elderly or disabled parent who is dependent on an adult child for support. This was the case for Cathy and Max. Although Max's children by his first marriage were grown-up and independent, the burden of Cathy's commitments had to be considered in the financial arrangements they made, when they married relatively late in life.

I still make payments to my mother who lives overseas. Obviously, this remained my responsibility when Max and I were married.

Supporting struts: additional income

Cathy was able to go on supporting her mother after her marriage to Max only because she continued to work—and because Max was prepared to help with the household chores.

The same is true for countless other couples. Where one partner has a previous family to maintain, two incomes may be an economic necessity. For others, however, the question of whether or not the wife should work is perhaps harder to resolve, as Barbara found out when she married Edward.

I just didn't know whether I should continue with my job or not. In many ways I didn't agree with working wives, and I felt it was important that I should be home when Edward got back. He works long hours and is physically drained at the end of the day. I didn't want not to be able to meet his needs because I was too tired myself.

Barbara also had two small girls from her first marriage to consider. Their needs and those of her new husband had to be weighed up against other conflicting factors: the fact that Edward had never been married before and might take some time to adjust; the financial and emotional constraints of having to take responsibility not only for his wife, but also for his two stepdaughters; the pressure of the precarious nature of his employment; and finally, the particularly low income that he earned at the time.

Edward insisted that the decision should be Barbara's as to whether or not she should continue with her job at the hospital. After talking it through with someone whose advice she trusted, Barbara decided that a compromise was needed and she asked for a temporary reduction in hours. Within a few weeks, changes in her department made that a feasible proposition, and she was soon reaping the benefit of a shorter working day, with more time and energy for her family. Edward, meanwhile, was very appreciative of the fact that he was spared the daunting financial responsibility of going from bachelor to sole provider in one stroke.

Answers to the following questions should help to establish the best solution for individual stepfamilies:

■ Will taking on a stepfamily put undue pressure upon the main breadwinner? Is there an economic necessity for two incomes?

■ Has remarriage brought about the loss of a pension or maintenance?

■ Does one partner have financial commitments (to a first family or elsewhere) that have to be met?

■ Are more children planned, adding to existing financial responsibilities?

■ Is paid employment seen as being desirable to the fulfilment of the wife, and therefore in the best interests of both partners?

■ Is the wife's job providing a service to the community that warrants being weighed up against the needs of the family?

One couple felt that this was a major factor in deciding that the wife should continue to work:

> *Lynn used her work as a district nurse to show God's love to a great many people—and she, in turn, was loved by her patients. We always had a bottom drawer full of chocs at Christmas time—given by them in appreciation of all she did.*

These days many women take it for granted that they will work whilst bringing up their families. But it wasn't always so. And there are still those who question the ethics of trying to master the juggling act demanded of working mothers. Is it really possible to keep all the balls in the air at once? Can they ever be all things to all people:

■ D.I.Y. enthusiasts, creating the right environment for the family; clothing and looking after them; shopping and cooking imaginatively economically; coping with the day to day demands of running a home—*and the delicate art of negotiating with husbands and children so as to delegate responsibility for at least some of the chores?*

■ good neighbours, able to practise hospitality; having the stamina to spend 'quality time' with them, with the family, with friends—listening to their problems and offering advice?

■ the super-efficient employee that the boss expects them to be (or running a business or cottage industry); balancing the household (and/or business) accounts?

■ and never (ever?) running out of steam!

Is it realistic to suppose that on top of all that anyone could expect them to be:

■ people who can look to the future, with a good grasp

of financial matters for today and tomorrow?

■ smart, attractive, and well-dressed; the supportive wife and alluring lover?

■ cool, calm and in control—and still allow time and space for both partners to be themselves?

Clearly the writer of the book of Proverbs in the Bible thought so when he chronicled the virtues of the 'Good Wife' who, by all accounts is worth more than precious gems!

> *She gets up before dawn to prepare breakfast for her household, and plans the day's work for her servants; works far into the night! is trustworthy and richly satisfies her husband's needs; sews for the poor and generously gives to the needy; is a woman of great strength and dignity; is never lazy; speaks wise words and is ruled by kindness; and, having no fear of old age, earns the praise and admiration of her children and husband, plus honour and recognition in the community.[14]*

Before there's an indignant outcry from women everywhere, or working mothers load themselves with guilt, let's take another look at one particular aspect of the story. The Good Wife in Proverbs took her responsibilities seriously—and first on her list each day was the responsibility of seeing that others played their part in the smooth running of the household. If we've never brought our children up to accept any sense of duty in this realm, then we're in for a tough time—and so are the people they ultimately marry!

It is outside the scope of this book to offer much in the way of advice on how to instil into children and teenagers, not simply a sense of obligation, but of pride, in taking their fair share of domestic responsibility. However, James Dobson has written several excellent books on the subject of discipline—working on the basis of a reward system. If we are not to nurture resentment in either ourselves (when the family suddenly doubles the day we remarry) or amongst individual members of the stepfamily (who may all have been brought up with a different set of values) it might be as well if we were to adopt some such procedure—and fast!

Set in concrete for future generations

Before we leave the inestimable qualities of the 'wife of noble character' let's consider, for a moment, her lack of concern for her old age and her provision for the 'winter' of her life. In order that we might have the same peace of mind that she enjoyed, we need to think about making a will.

Some couples choose to see a solicitor in this respect before they remarry. The wills of each partner can then be held by the Registrar pending the ceremony—at which time they may be signed, together with the marriage certificate (using the same witnesses for both) so that they come into effect immediately. If you think that is carrying caution to extremes, just ponder on how often fatal accidents are reported in the newspapers as having occurred whilst bride and groom are travelling to, or from, their honeymoon destination, or when indulging in some sort of holiday activity whilst there.

Incorporating the signing of wills into the marriage ceremony means that there is less likelihood of their being put off until some nebulous date in the future. It also has the advantage that both partners know exactly where they stand from the outset, as regards provision for their own future, that of their partner and, perhaps more importantly, for the children of each.

Additionally, certain safeguards can be included to ensure that our wishes are interpreted accurately, and carried out as we intend them to be. For instance, the manner in which the purchase of a house is set up may considerably limit (or safeguard) the manner of its disposal—both during life and after death. In this respect, it's vital to understand the difference in English law between being joint tenants and tenants in common.

Joint tenants—whereby each owns 100 per cent of the house

Advantages:

■ neither can sell up without the other's signed consent

■ on the death of one partner, the house (complete with mortgage repayments unless an endowment has been taken out to settle the repayments) automatically becomes the property of the other—even if there is no will

■ if anything goes wrong with the relationship, either may serve notice on the other at any time that they are 'severing the joint tenancy'

Disadvantages:

■ Because, on your death, your partner is free to leave the property as he or she wishes, your children will not necessarily stand to inherit any part of it—even if you had money invested in it.

This could be of particular relevance if your partner marries again after your death. The new husband/wife may take precedence over your children—with or without a will being made.

It is vital, therefore, that your will incorporates a trust, in order that your children will inherit your share in the property on the death of your spouse. In this respect, a solicitor's advice should be sought.

Tenants in common—whereby each owns a percentage of the home (say 50–50)

Advantages:

■ You own outright (and theoretically may sell) your share in the house if the marriage breaks down

■ You are also free to will your share directly to your children (as your partner may will his/her share to your stepchildren)

Disadvantages:

■ In theory (and perhaps in practice) one partner could sell his/her share without the consent of the other

■ Neither you (nor your partner) automatically owns the property on the death of the other. Making a will therefore becomes paramount

■ However, a will may be changed at any time with or without your knowledge. This means that (technically, at least) you could find yourself homeless

■ Because the children/stepchildren may inherit half the property on the death of one partner, this could be putting power in their hands to evict the other (or at least attempt to). A 'Right to Reside' clause should be inserted to guard against this.

■ Trustees should also be empowered to sell the house on the instruction of the surviving partner, in order that he/she might realize their own capital and/or purchase a new property. A solicitor will advise.

Most couples choose to make some sort of provision for the offspring of a previous marriage, though the manner and extent to which this is done varies enormously. When Lynn married Frank, she owned the lion's share of their combined total assets. Both felt that it was only right and proper, therefore, that she should have first claim on the estate (all the money and possessions owned by the deceased) in the event of Frank's death. Even so, they chose to make provision for Frank's daughters, in addition to his divorce settlement.

> *Lynn and I agreed that I should make a token legacy for my two girls.*

Dawn and John dealt with things rather differently—in a way that was more in keeping with their situation.

> *We've each left one third to each of our own children, and one third to each other. But we've appointed trustees so that the children can't 'blow it'. The money is to be distributed gradually during the years between their twenty-first birthdays and when they're thirty-five.*

For other couples, the whole question appears to be too fraught to bear consideration. Some seem to be tempted to 'leave it all to God', in a way that displays a woolly, sentimentalized 'faith' that is not faith at all, but a travesty of the sort of trust the Bible advocates. Playing the ostrich and burying our heads in the sand is simply to renege on our responsibilities. In effect, we merely defer the headaches until later, and may actually, by dying intestate (without a will), offload enormous burdens onto our dependants.

The fact is that dying intestate may mean that our estate is 'frozen' (unable to be used) until the relevant authorities have assessed the duty, or tax, to be paid. Depending on the complexity of the estate (privately owned business, partnership, stocks and shares, properties other than the main residence, endowments and life assurance, as well as jewellery and all the usual personal possessions) this could take months. Even years! Then, to add insult to injury, the person or persons we intended should inherit may not do so at all. As Colin found out.

My mother died when I was in my late teens. I don't think she left a will, so naturally, everything went to my father. He then remarried and for a while I lived at home. Though I was never what you would call close to my stepmother—I think she always felt a bit jealous of the relationship I had with my dad—we got on well enough.

When Dad and my stepmother made wills twenty years later, they left everything to each other, on the understanding that it would then go to my brother and me. But after my father's death, my stepmother promptly changed her will and left the lion's share to someone who wasn't even a relation of hers.

I think she would have liked to cut my brother and me out completely, though we'd all maintained normal family relationships even after Dad's death. But I suspect that she took advice and was told that if she did so, we might have taken the matter to court. After all, some of what my father had left her had once belonged to my real mother.

The money would have come in useful—especially to my brother who suffered a terminal illness for eight years before he died, too. But what really upset me was the fact that my real mother had placed her trust in my father to see us right, and he had then trusted my stepmother to keep her word, and she'd ultimately broken that trust.

Colin is not the only one to find the intentions of one or both of his parents flouted by a misplaced trust in the step-parent. But even where this is not the case, deep resentments can take root in adult offspring who see their childhood home (which had once been inhabited by both their natural parents before the death of one and remarriage of the other) left to the step-parent and possibly his/her children. This is par-ticularly true of the children of a widowed parent who has remarried late in life. A stepmother, in such cases, may actually be little older (if at all) than her stepchildren.

This whole area is fraught. Naturally enough, you want to provide for your partner and children—but which ones should that be? The Bible is quite unequi-vocal on the matter.

> *If a man has two wives, and he loves one but not the other, and both bear him sons but the firstborn is the son of the wife he does not love, when he wills his property to his sons, he must not give the rights of the firstborn to the son of the wife he loves in preference to his actual firstborn, the son of the wife he does not love. He must acknowledge the son of his unloved wife as the firstborn by giving him a double share of all he has. That son is the first sign of his father's strength. The right of the firstborn belongs to him.*[15]

Although couched in somewhat quaint and sexist terms, the principles espoused in this text have a relevance that is as fresh and meaningful as when it was written several thousand years ago. 'Firstborn sons' may not have quite the significance that they once had when it comes to signifying a father's strength—nor be deserving of in-heriting a 'double share'! But the morals of making provision for the children of a wife who has 'fallen from favour' can be thought no less valid for all that.

7

Forming a Framework

You have to give this much to the Luftwaffe—when it knocked down our buildings it did not replace them with anything more offensive than rubble. We did that.

CHARLES, PRINCE OF WALES

If we are not to be guilty of doing the same thing with our families, then we need to understand that the relationship between husband and wife, parent and step-parent, is the framework upon which the whole family/stepfamily structure is built. If anything is askew in this area, it throws all the other members out of kilter with one another. We may not be aware of the effects but, seen or unseen, we may be sure that they will be eating away like death watch beetle or dry rot at the security of the children we're attempting to raise. Their future stability rests upon us, their parents and step-parents.

It follows, therefore, that having cleared away the debris of damaged emotions and laid down firm foundations in terms of winning the respect of prospective stepchildren, the next priority is to see that the framework we establish in the early days of remarriage will be robust enough to carry the weight of building the whole new set of relationships that form the stepfamily.

What we're after is not simply to replace the 'demolished' fragmented family with something similar. The aim is to improve upon the past, with all its problems and pain. And to do that, we need to learn from our mistakes, make every decision count, and build upon our strengths. One strength which is paramount is to recognize our limitations and those of our partner. We need to hold to realistic expectations.

Revealing the rough edges of regret

It is a false premise to expect that any marriage can ever answer *all* our needs. To think otherwise is totally unrealistic and is doomed to disappointment. And this, perhaps, is one of the prime reasons for the failure of so many marriages.

False expectations can lead a man to believe that his wife should be all things to him: chief cook and bottle washer, social and administrative secretary, nanny and chauffeuse and, above all, an alluring and willing sex-siren—without help, and at all times of the day or night. To all such errant husbands, James Dobson, eminent psychiatrist and prolific writer, has plenty to say in his excellent books and videos on Family Focus.

Having chastised men for their insensitivity and work-oriented—rather than relationship-oriented—priorities, he then turns his attention to the women. Wives with good, steady, but busy and noncommunicative husbands cannot expect to depend upon them to feed their emotional starvation, he says. This is because they may be quite unable to do so. Unable! Not unwilling. His solution is for women to look to other women for the emotional support they need.

In different cultures and times, this happened quite

naturally—in marriage preparation; in midwifery; in dressing the dead; and in everyday tasks like doing the laundry at the riverside; fetching water from the well; buying and selling at the marketplace. However, with the rites of passage now largely male-dominated, the advent of career women, and a general demise in community, women have become far more isolated. Time spent with other women often has to be contrived.

In addition, marriage itself has changed. With greater equality and companionship, our feeling is that it's somehow 'wrong' or 'disloyal' to expect some of our needs to be met by anyone other than our spouse. Rather than accept that this is a fabrication, when those needs go unmet we tend to believe that this was due to some failure in either our partner or ourselves. 'If only I'd been more...this or that,' we say. Or, 'if only he/she had been more... attentive... sexy... sociable...'

For those of us to whom remarriage is a reality, there is the temptation of thinking: *this time*... 'This time,' we determine, 'it will all come right.' This time both partners are... older and wiser... richer or slimmer... more successful, less ambitious. We've had our 'colours done'; our teeth capped; or we've learned to drive. This time we know what we want in marriage. And we'll 'get' what we want from the relationship.

But the truth is that 'this time' can only happen if *we've* changed our way of thinking; if we're 'giving' as good as we're 'getting' (in terms of loving, caring, forgiving) and understand the fine-tuning between the two. This time, we need to be sure that we've attracted and selected a partner who is *totally different from the first*. Because if *we* haven't changed in what we look for in a partner, then two, five or ten years down the line, we may find that, though we've presented ourselves with a new 'lead' actor or actress, we're in fact following the same old script, playing out the same old plot—with the same unmodified characters. As Carol discovered—just in time.

> *After a few years of being on my own, I realized that I seemed to be gravitating towards men who were exactly like my ex-husband—business men who were macho, ambitious and successful. Suddenly I woke up to the fact that most were also predatory, sexist and had little interest in home life except when it suited. So when I met Gavin who was completely the opposite, I thought: Wonderful!*
>
> *To begin with it was. Wonderful, I mean. I used to tease him that in the first few years of our marriage we spent more time in DIY superstores than anywhere else—but the fact was that I was thrilled to have a husband who enjoyed doing things around the house. It was something we could do together.*

Gavin was an intensely practical man. He'd bottled up his feelings for years because that was how he'd been brought up—but that wasn't too much of a problem. Carol was quite skilled in counselling and knew how to draw him out. For his part, he was always willing to talk and explore the things that were important to their relationship. And he was affectionate in a quiet way.

> *The trouble came when the money and euphoria of getting our home together ran out, and we had less to occupy us together. I found myself wanting him to be more masterful; more dynamic. He would always fall in with any suggestions I made—such as having a romantic meal out (or in)—but he found it very difficult to take a lead in such things.*

Carol began to feel exasperated when Gavin wouldn't take a lead in things outside the home, either. She started to criticize him and to feel slightly resentful that it always had to be her who made the first move. The more negative she felt, the less appealing his good traits appeared. His thrifty nature—which she'd applauded after the profligacy of her ex-husband—now began to look mean. His caution —which she'd once welcomed as security—became boring. Secretly she began to pick flaws in him.

> Then one day I woke up to the fact that I had no right to be judgmental, and that I was actually working against myself. Against what I wanted of my marriage.

> I had to remind myself that I fell in love with Gavin precisely because he was a gentle homeloving sort of person. I knew he couldn't be those things and be the other things I thought I wanted him to be. If he wasn't very ambitious in his job then that was all to the good because it meant we had more time together. And if he wasn't very good at the romantic things— taking me out, or buying me gifts—then at least I could be thankful that neither was he chatting up other women, lavishing his mistresses with expensive presents, or buying things for me just as a sop to his conscience. All of which I'd had to endure in my first marriage.

Gradually, Carol began to wonder if perhaps some of the reason why Gavin stayed in a nice safe job on the bottom rung was because he lacked confidence. She came to believe, through prayer and reflection, that if she built him up and encouraged him, he'd be less cautious. Less fearful of doing the wrong thing. She hadn't bargained for quite how well it would work!

> He started his own business a few years ago—something he would never have had the nerve to do before. But he's still the same nice easy man I married. And though I'd still like him to be a bit more demonstrative in his affection, and to instigate a few romantic elements in our lives, I feel safe and secure with him. I think I've learned to appreciate that it's precisely because of his good points that he is as he is. You can't be gentle and homeloving and dynamic and ambitious, can you?

Sanding down for a smooth surface

When the honeymoon period had worn off for Carol, she'd had to reach a particular point of understanding— an admission of her unrealistic expectations, and a willingness to change her own way of thinking—even if there was no corresponding change in Gavin.

She was fortunate. In some respects Gavin changed quite dramatically—responding well to the encouragement she had shown him. She has learned to appreciate his finer points. However, she has also had to learn to accept that in some areas he will never change; not because he doesn't want to, but because he is consti-tutionally unable to do so. Quite simply, it isn't in his nature to be 'dynamic'.

Unless we can make these sort of allowances for one another and aim for harmony in our marriage, then we have no hope of achieving harmony in the family.

Personally, I've always thought that marriage is rather like the stone-polisher my eldest daughter was once given for her birthday. She would gather together pebbles from the beach, bits of broken glass and old beads, pour in water and a coarse grit, seal the top, then set the little machine tumbling day and night. Endlessly it would grind away at the rough edges of the stones.

After a week or more of intensive friction, they would be taken out, relatively smooth but far from shiny, rinsed and returned to the machine. A finer sand would then be added and the whole process repeated over and over again—with progressively finer grades of abrasive— until eventually the stones emerged crystal clear and finely honed. From an unpromising start those rough, lacklustre bits of rock would become gemstones of outstanding beauty.

I'm not suggesting that we're meant to knock lumps off each other (that's what actually happens in a bad marriage). Quite the reverse. The essential ingredient in that little stone polisher was the various grades of scouring and buffing material: the refiner. In the case of marriage, we have one refining material: love. Its various grades include the four c's:

■ commitment to starting over, each and every time we feel like jacking it all in

■ communication between each partner

■ contrition: (willingness to admit we're in the wrong)

■ conciliation (letting our partner off the hook when he/she is in the wrong).

And for Christians, the four c's operate not only between us and our partner, but between us and God.

However laborious the process of 'rubbing along together', however painful the abrasive nature of our partnership at times, it can actually be to our mutual benefit. But only if we can each say with total honesty: I will allow this conflict to be the means of refining *me*.

It all depends on our sense of commitment; our willingness to submit ourselves to the 'treatment'. But if it is our desire to have the rough edges of our personalities smoothed, to be moulded and refined, then marriage is an excellent stone-polisher to make us into gemstones. The treatment is quite simple. It consists of:

■ handling conflict in a constructive manner by allowing a cooling-off period, then choosing the right moment to sit down and talk together.

■ committing ourselves to taking it in turns for each of us to have a short period of sharing our feelings—uninterrupted by the other

■ listening, feeding back what we think we've heard, then being prepared to listen again if we discover we've misunderstood what our partner is saying

■ not pointing the finger at our partners and making accusations, but asking for help with our unmet needs. '*I* have a problem... can you help me?' is a much better opening for pointing out our inability to cope with certain omissions or patterns of behaviour on the part of our partner than an irritable: '*You* make me mad...'

■ brainstorming; using lateral thinking to arrive at solutions that don't necessarily have to involve capitulation (one giving in to the other) or compromise (both giving in, neither getting what they want); but co-existence (an alternative decision that pleases both equally)

■ allowing our own entrenched ideas to be changed (of how 'things' should be done; of what we expect from ourselves, our partner, our marriage)

■ accepting new priorities in our thinking and behaviour (in terms of how we apportion our time, our physical and mental endeavour, our money; my job versus domestic responsibilities; my own leisure pursuits versus the emotional and spiritual needs of my family)

■ encouraging our partner's strengths through praise and admiration

■ recognizing and building up our partner in their weak points

■ working on our own weaknesses

■ valuing our partners—vocally and demonstrably.

To achieve all this we need to create time to be alone together; time when we can learn to communicate effectively; time simply to enjoy one another. Unfortunately, in a stepfamily, that may be the one commodity we're most lacking.

Carving out communication

Unlike a first marriage, remarriage often comes with a ready-made family: stepchildren of perhaps widely divergent ages and interests. Whereas first-time newly-weds can look forward to a period of relative solitude with one another before the arrival of a third person in the household, that may be a luxury which is unavailable to those embarking on a second marriage.

Years of evenings filled with children may lie ahead before we have the opportunity to indulge in an uninterrupted conversation with our partner. Evenings of nagging about bedtimes and tidying rooms; of holding our breath, of biting the bullets and clenching our fists lest we explode, as we struggle to get our minds, energies, time and emotions around the hazards of exams, drugs and teenage pregnancies.

Can there be anything more unsatisfactory than a row with our partner which has to be left hanging in the air by the arrival of an adolescent on the scene? Or a rare stolen moment of joy which is swiftly and rudely terminated by the intrusion of a cold and pathetic little figure between us in the bed? Or an outing curtailed by wails of: 'I feel s..i...ck...' from upstairs, as we're about to fetch the babysitter?

All parents have to endure these things. But the point

is that most have at least nine months and however many years in which to become acclimatized to parenthood. For those who have never been married before, never shared a house with a teenager, never seen the workings of a family, the shock may be immense. Chris had been tight-lipped for some time before Pam eventually got him to admit:

> It's Sarah. I just find her so incredibly rude in the mornings. I say 'Good morning' to her and all I get is a grunt—at best! I know it shouldn't bother me. I've tried to tell myself to let it go. But I just can't stand it any longer. Even the kids at school don't treat me like that, with such indifference.

Pam could see that there were complex issues of false expectation that needed to be talked out, and that although almost all the solutions involved Chris seeing things differently, she had to be diplomatic and non-judgmental in how she put it across. First of all she spoke to Sarah, pointing out that though she wasn't used to having a man about the house, now that she was entering puberty she really had to make an effort to be a little more presentable—both physically and verbally. Having done so, she was then able to tell Chris that she'd had a word with her daughter. This, in turn, had the effect of placating him and making him more open to what she had to say next—as she recounts:

> The thing is that neither Chris nor Sarah are at their best in the mornings. They both come alive later on. They're night owls. Consequently, when they met on the landing first thing in the morning, they were both feeling pretty disgruntled at having to cope with something that was new and strange to them—at a time of the day when they were not really in the right frame of mind to do so.

Besides that, it had never occurred to Chris that when he faced a class of children at school he did so as their teacher— not as someone who had recently taken up residence with their mother. They were bound to be polite and well-mannered, because he was a figure of authority to them. They weren't emotionally involved with him in the way that Sarah was.

On top of that, he was seeing them a couple of hours down the line—at morning assembly. He'd no idea what they would have been like at seven am, dragged from their warm beds...

There was no need for Pam to say any more. Chris was reasonable enough to see that what she said made sense. In future, he and Sarah made no attempt to comply with conventional morning greetings, but confined their breakfast-time conversation to the minimum. By the end of the day, when Pam (a morning lark) was longing to wind down, the two night-owls—stepfather and stepdaughter— were in fine fettle, and made it known that they had no intention of allowing her to sink into apathy!

Pam and Chris discovered that if they spent time talking through the issues of each day when they retired to bed—the one place they could give each other their undivided attention—the closeness that this brought about in their feelings for one another actually had the effect of enhancing their sex-life.

We made a commitment to one another that we would never say anything destructive about each other. If ever we're in danger of . doing that in the heat of a row during the day, we just walk away to the proverbial 'potting-shed'. For Chris that's usually the garden or the garage. For me—I might go for a walk.

Then we have a sharing time later. Often that has to be in bed. We try to hold hands and maintain eye-contact. Telling each other our deepest feelings—and fears—seems to bring us closer. Quite often we end up making love—and it always seems better than at any other time.

Of course, it doesn't always work like that—and sometimes, especially at the 'wrong' time of the month, I find myself goading Chris. What I'm actually longing for is for him to put his arms around me. But by the time it's got to that stage, it's often the last thing in the world that Chris feels able to do. Fortunately, neither of us can bear to go to sleep until we've cleared the air. In the early days of our marriage, one way or the other, we had a lot of sleepless nights...

The problem of finding opportunities to be able to communicate more effectively with our partners can be resolved in different ways. Some methods work. Others leave one or other feeling dissatisfied. Frequently, it proves more difficult for the parent—who tends to grapple with feelings of guilt about 'neglecting' the children—than it is for the step-parent. As Terry recounts:

Time alone with Isobel—that's something we disagree about. I feel we put the children first too often. We should sometimes say 'this is what we're doing'—and let them get on with it. After all, in a few years time we'll be on our own and just have each other. We've got to build a relationship now.

Terry and Isobel eventually converted a bedroom so that if they had people in, or merely wanted time alone, the girls had somewhere to watch TV with their friends.

When Steve and Ruth found they had a problem in this respect, they felt that the occasional evening out together was the best way for them to tackle the issue.

Creating time together—that's been more of a problem of late, with the children getting older... We always know when we've neglected each other. A sort of dryness creeps in. I've had to learn to communicate with Ruth.

Steve used to come home, eat, help me get the kids to bed and then we would just want to flop in front of the telly. Our lives never got interwoven.

I'm old-fashioned—protecting the 'little wife' from the problems and pressures of business—and I felt there was a loss of manliness if I talked to her. But I know it really helps... We're really lucky having Ruth's mum to relieve us [to babysit]. She's the best mother-in-law I've had!

With two others to choose from, he should know!

Some of the principles used in this book are based on those of Marriage Enrichment Classes. Making a commitment to attend a two-hour class each week over a period of approximately six weeks was the way that Paul and I chose to focus our attention on each other and on our marriage. The skills we learned during exercises conducted as individuals, couples, and small groups have stood us in good stead over the years—and we later went on to run classes. Topics covered included:

■ The creative use of conflict (what irritates; conflict resolution)

■ positive sharing (I am happiest with you when... what I look forward to most in the future with you is...)

■ listening and hearing (showing appreciation; styles of communication; hearing and understanding)

■ intimacy and independence (three things that: I like about our relationship; could be even better; I could do to make it better)

■ striking bargains (ways of negotiating)

■ three essentials for good coupling (what do I want for me/for you/for us?)

■ making contracts (commitment about specific issues)

Other organizations offer weekend residential courses.

And for those who tremble at the thought of small-group dynamics, there are classes which concentrate on individual, written exercises, which are later shared only partner-to-partner.

I might once have put myself in this category—and Paul certainly would have done. What we found, however, was that much of the benefit for us came in learning from other couples during small-group sessions. Sharing takes place whilst seated in a circle, and each individual shares with the others only to the extent that he/she wishes. It was liberating (and amusing) to discover that certain foibles and failings (the things that mildly irritated us about the other) were not peculiar to us, but seemed to be gender-related and were, therefore, encountered quite widely.

The experience, as well as being fun, actually lived up to its promise to enrich our marriage—in more ways than one. It opened our eyes to the reasons behind some of the areas of dissatisfaction in our relationship—and, most importantly, furnished us with the wherewithal to deal with them effectively. In addition, it provided us with the pleasure of new friends who have now become old friends.

In an era when people are looking for diversionary tactics as a means of escape from unfulfilled lives, we would not hesitate to recommend this method as one of the best for enjoying quality time together. Why should we be so ready to attend evening classes in cookery, languages, art, ballroom dancing... yet so slow to take the opportunity to learn about each other?

Dovetailing the old with the new

The delicate subject of whether or not we are free to talk about the past is one of those issues that is best resolved early on. Dawn has met John's first wife. Privately she finds it incomprehensible that Zoe could ever have left her children when she walked out on John. However, she feels that for their sakes (as well as his) she must be able to talk naturally about their mother. In addition, she knows she must be prepared to allow them the freedom to show old photographs or talk about events which happened long before she came on the scene.

> *John said to me: 'If there's anything you want to say about your past, or pass comment on about mine, just say it.' If he wants to say anything, I wouldn't be jealous or resentful, because we're the ones living together now.*

John's and Dawn's attitudes show a healthy realism. No parent, step-parent or stepchild can be expected to behave as if they have no past. A good many of the anecdotes that form part of any normal conversation between friends and family may have occurred in the period prior to a remarriage. Such things, if we're the well-balanced, emotionally-healed people we're aiming to be, should incite no more jealousy or insecurity than those of a first marriage. To reiterate what Dawn had to say: 'We're the ones living together now.' Perhaps we need to remind ourselves of that, if ever the green-eyed monster of jealousy threatens our security?

Open-plan living?

Another potentially thorny issue is whether or not we should be openly affectionate in front of the children. One mother spoke of her daughter timing every embrace that she had with her new husband, then comparing the result unfavourably with that of the hugs she herself received. They had not yet resolved the matter—unlike Pam and Chris, for whom this was one of the topics of their nocturnal sharing sessions.

> *I am naturally a very tactile person. All my family hug and kiss each other. But when Chris and I got married, Sarah used to kick up a fuss if she walked in and found us having a hug. Chris felt we should make a point of not showing any affection to one another in front of her because he didn't want to upset her. But I said I thought she'd grow up with a very odd idea of marriage if she saw us keeping each other at arm's length all the time.*
>
> *In the end, we just used to lift our arms up and include her in the hug—which she hated. But I used to turn it into a joke, and after a while she came around. She still doesn't like being hugged by Chris. But now, if she walks in on us, she just teases—says something like: 'Oh the honeymoon couple!' or 'Snogging again!' But it's all in good humour, and it's obvious that our affection no longer challenges her feelings of security.*

Some couples would be horrified with the policy that Chris and Pam adopted. They are adamant in opposing any display of feelings which might conceivably risk upsetting their own children or their stepchildren, and believe that affection, like arguments, should be kept behind closed doors. Alan and Val disagree.

> *Children's needs vary. My youngest daughter is like her father—not very demonstrative. But my eldest is naturally affectionate like me. Actually, Mary used to embarrass Alan when we first got married. He wasn't used to being given a full-frontal hug by a nubile young woman, and eventually I had to point that out to her—very tactfully. I think she understood. She's just as affectionate as she ever was. But now it's in a way that he can cope with.*

Peter and Sandra had similar problems. Peter recalls that his eldest stepdaughter was very possessive to begin with.

> *If I showed any affection to Sandra, Olivia used to say things like: 'Take your arm off my mummy. She's my mummy.'*

Peter was very concerned that Olivia should not feel that he was taking everything away from her and, for a while, it affected relationships all round. Every time Peter tried to assert an air of authority, there was a kick-back from Olivia, and it upset Sandra. Eventually, it was Peter's natural exuberance and genuine affection for his stepdaughters that persuaded Olivia that she had nothing to fear. Unfortunately, however, she over-responded.

> *She'd missed out on the normal pre-puberty relationship with her father, and it was as if she hadn't had chocolate cake before and now wanted to gorge herself. She hung all over me. It got embarrassing for everyone.*

> *We had to explain to her that she was growing up. Rather than reject her for being all over Peter when we came home from work, he used to turn her to me and say: 'Go and give your mum a cuddle first.' She'd cooled down a bit then by the time she got back to Peter.*

So much for keeping parental affection under wraps. When it came to concealing arguments from the children, Val had more to say.

> *I think they have to learn that in the real world people do argue. Even people who love each other. The important thing is that they realize marriage isn't a bed of roses—but neither is a row inevitably going to lead to divorce. They have to learn that disagreements can be resolved, and to understand that, they need to see it in practice.*

Dawn agrees.

*Once when John and I had a row, it was Amy that made us
sit down and talk things out.*

Amy had learned two important points from her earlier
encounter when she'd accused her mother of having an
affair with John. The first was the necessity of a cooling
off period, when she'd moved to her grandparents. The
second was the value of discerning communication.

At that time, Dawn had looked beyond Amy's rudeness,
and realized that it was insecurity that was governing her
behaviour. She'd recognized this as being due to a
combination of events: the death of her daughter's father;
the betrayal of the unscrupulous man with whom Dawn
had subsequently become involved; and finally, the loss of
her sister's companionship when she'd married.
Communication between mother and daughter had led to
understanding, and understanding to reconciliation.

The experience had evidently stuck in Amy's mind.
Consequently, when John and Dawn reached an impasse
after a major row—a row conducted in Amy's presence
rather than behind closed doors—she'd been able to
remind them of the need for effective communication.
With their differences resolved, their openness as a
family proved to be of benefit all round.

8

Brickwork and Building Techniques

There will, inevitably, be a fresh rawness in new step-families that will take time to mellow. Reaching a state of comfortable familiarity will be an ongoing learning experience; a learning curve which, obviously, will be easiest for those families who have put in the most amount of preparation prior to the wedding. Step-families like Isobel's and Terry's.

Asked whether he ever felt the odd one out, Terry replied:

> *Not really—no. When their [Isobel's daughters'] bikes needed fixing, it was me they came to. And I had to build cages for the rabbits and so on.*

Or Steve's and Ruth's:

> *Tracey was too young ever to remember a time when I wasn't in her life, but Kevin reacted. He was very 'anti' his mother. He was on his dad's side. There's always been a special relationship between Steve and Kevin. I moved in (two years prior to their marriage) to see if I could accept Tracey and Kevin as my own children.*

> *Kevin knew he was better off. Ruth was a much better mother than Yvonne.*

Cementing together

For those members of a stepfamily who have had less time to get to know one another, those first few months of living under the same roof can be make or break. Alan, who had been so concerned on Hannah's behalf prior to his marriage to Val, found his stepdaughter's reaction quite puzzling to begin with.

> *Every night when I got home from work she'd be waiting for me—hiding in the hallway. Then she'd jump out, and be all over me: demanding to be 'walked' on my feet, or just treating me like a climbing frame. It was quite bizarre. The sort of behaviour you'd expect from a small child, not a thirteen-year-old.*

He found Hannah's attentions quite amusing. But it wasn't until he talked it through with Val that, between them, they were able to shed some light on her daughter's childish behaviour.

> *She was quite young when her father left. We realized that she must have been reverting to the behaviour of a seven-year-old simply because she didn't know how else to behave with a man in a family situation.*

Hannah continued to find it difficult to know how to relate to her stepfather. It was perfectly obvious that she wanted to have some sort of tactile relationship with him, but was prevented from doing so by her own inhibitions. Hence her resort to horseplay. As she grew a little older and more familiar with Alan, she changed the metaphor. Instead of treating him like a climbing frame, he became her Action Man.

> *She began by going through his wardrobe and telling him she wouldn't be seen dead with him in the seventies bell-bottoms and platform shoes he'd hoarded for years, but never wore. I*

wouldn't have dared throw them out. He would never have taken it from me. But he didn't seem to mind with Hannah, and agreed to part with them.

Then she started choosing the shirt and tie she thought he should wear if he and I were going out together. She'd even want to tie his tie. And from there, she would tell me what clothes I should buy for him. 'Get him these trousers, Mummy. He does need new ones, you know, and these are really hip and trendy.'

Alan, who could never previously have been described as 'hip and trendy', was delighted—not only with his new image, but with his burgeoning relationship with his stepdaughter. Although, very occasionally, he found Hannah's childishness a little irksome, for the most part he thoroughly enjoyed her attentions—especially when she turned to trimming his hair. Val was as pleased as Alan.

After a while, he began to ask her to do it for him whenever the back got a bit straggly. He'd never have trusted me. But I'm glad, because it's given the two of them something from which I'm excluded.

Carol and Gavin found a similar approach to the relationships in their family.

Gavin found that my youngest daughter just wouldn't respond at all to begin with. If he asked her if she'd like to do something or other she was very negative. So he decided to stop asking. Instead, he'd just drop it out that he had tickets for the football match—and lo and behold! his psychology worked. She'd be quite put out that he hadn't asked her.

She loves football—it's something she and Gavin have in common. When she discovered how little I knew about the subject, she started putting me down—only in a teasing, sort of 'nudge-nudge, wink-wink, look how dumb Mum is' thing with Gavin. I suppose I could have been quite hurt. But I

wasn't. On the contrary. I was so pleased that they had
something going for them that didn't include me that I
actually played up to it—acted dumber than I really was.

Too many foremen, not enough brickies?

Good-humouredly, Carol and Gavin began developing
their strategy. She continued to 'play up' to the situation.
He was cool and 'laid back', allowing Natalie to come to
him instead of pushing himself at her—until eventually,
a genuine rapport existed between stepdaughter and
stepfather.

In the wake of their success, Carol began to see other
aspects of their relationship in a new light, and to feel
that they, too, could benefit from a little subtle influence.
For instance, establishing Gavin, in Natalie's mind, as
someone whose opinions were worthy of respect—
someone to be looked up to—was not going to happen
naturally overnight.

I found that she was constantly coming to me to make
decisions. Or asking me to give my permission for her to do
something or other. For instance, whenever she wanted to
make a phone call she'd ask me. Or could she put the fire on
because she was 'frozen'. When you've been the main
breadwinner for so long, I suppose it's only natural. But I
wanted her to start seeing Gavin as the provider and figure
of authority in her life...

Each time that Natalie asked her mother to make a
decision or give permission about anything, Carol began
referring her to Gavin. Or she, herself, would say: 'Is it
all right with you, Gavin, if Natalie does...'

To begin with, it was obvious that Natalie believed
that Gavin was usurping her mother's place as the

'oracle' in her life. But gradually, as Carol reinforced his position in the family with gentle reminders that it was now him who took care of them and paid the domestic bills, not her, Natalie was able to accept the status quo. At no time did Gavin himself ever attempt to underline what Carol was doing, though he gave her actions his tacit approval.

> *I felt it was important not to chip in. You could so easily sound like a martyr saying: 'It's not up to your mother; I pay the phone bill now.'*

Nor did he ever offer unsolicited advice—a fact that was noted and appreciated by one of his other stepdaughters when she came to stay for a while.

> *Dad's wife drives me mad. She never stops going on: 'You should do this' or: 'Your father thinks it would be best if...' as if she knows him better than I do. My friend's stepdad's even worse. He never lets up. They have awful rows when he goes on about what she should be doing—and her mum supports him against her. I'm glad Gavin's not like that.*

There can be no hard and fast rules when it comes to establishing a step-parent as an authority in the family. Respect has to be earned, and the process cannot be hastened. Some parents want to establish their new partner instantly in a parental role; others find it difficult to relinquish control themselves. When disagreements occur between stepchild and step-parent (or stepchild and stepchild) it can be incredibly difficult for the natural parent to take an objective view. Split loyalties make demands on both sides. Are we to support our spouse's reasoned, adult argument? Or is this a betrayal of the impassioned pleas of our own offspring? If we take a major role in 'helping things along' will this simply exacerbate the situation? Should we abandon them to sort the thing out without interference from us? Gavin feels humour has played a significant role in defusing potentially explosive situations in his household.

> *If ever it got too 'heavy', we'd turn it into a joke. Carol would say something about the 'wicked stepfather' or something like that. Sometimes Natalie would react in a cross way, but it usually worked in the end.*

When it came to taking on the role of disciplinarian, Terry, who had already established a good relationship with his stepdaughters, had no qualms.

> *I filled the gap their father left. I went for that. I didn't sit back and wait for that to happen. I think I've behaved as a normal parent would. If they've needed discipline, I've disciplined them.*
>
> *I don't mind looking an idiot. Messing around. Having fun. So it balances out. If there was any problem it was with Isobel having to take a back seat. She didn't always agree with what I've done.*
>
> *I've never disagreed with Terry in front of the children. I don't think he always thinks a punishment through. Going to bed at 6pm every night for a fortnight puts tremendous strain on all the family.*
>
> *Yes. That's one of my faults. I tend to stick to what I've decided and won't back down. I won't put up with insolence. Once when the eldest was going on about her father I said: 'Right! If he's so terrific, go and live with him.' She was really shocked because she knew I meant it. So I dialled the number and she spoke to him...*

As Isobel recalls it, her ex-husband was equally shocked to think he might have to have their daughter to live

with him. The girl had been making life pretty un-
bearable for them all.

> *But things got better by the minute, because she knew we
> would have carried it out.*

This sort of threat can work in one family, yet backfire in
another.

We are all grappling with one of the greatest periods of
confusion, uncertainty and instability the Western world
has ever known. Since the Second World War, the whole
concept of authority has been steadily eroded. As a result,
we have seen the ethos of family life (amongst other things)
in decline, whilst at the same time there has been an
increase in crime, and in stress-related illness.

We are now living with the absurdity of, on the one
hand, a 'no-smacking' directive from the Charter of
Children's Rights in Brussels and, on the other, an
attempt by our own government to lower the age at
which young offenders may be prosecuted. Not
surprisingly, parents and step-parents alike, are in a
state of confusion.

It is at this point that tried and trusted principles
offer the only sort of yardstick worth measuring up to. I
have already mentioned James Dobson's books on discipline, and I do not hesitate to do so again. Based on
the teaching of the Bible, they expound sound methods
of training children to fulfil their potential through the
development of self-discipline. In the meantime, I leave
you with these statements:

> *Train a child in the way he should go, and when he is old he
> will not turn from it.*[16]

> *He who spares the rod hates his son, but he who loves him is
> careful to discipline him.*[17]

Fathers, do not exasperate your children; instead, bring them up in the training and instruction of the Lord.[18]

Investment in your workforce

The desire to establish a 'normal' family is so strong on the part of some parents or step-parents that it can be overwhelming. The fact is that it will only work if it is neither forced nor contrived. We've already seen from Alan's experience (Chapter 5) that adolescent children who are expected to call a step-parent 'Mum' or 'Dad' from the moment of their parent's remarriage often feel uncomfortable—even rebellious.

The same may be true of children who are coerced into having to kiss a step-parent goodnight, or to embrace them when circumstances dictate a parting or coming together again. This sort of pressure can be a cruel form of torture to a particularly sensitive child, especially if it occurs in the vulnerable period immediately pre-pubescence.

Another more subtle form of pressure is that of the step-parent who plies a child with gifts or expensive outings. This may be self-instigated, or at the direction of the natural parent. It may be the result of manipulative behaviour on the part of parent or step-parent, or merely indicative of their insecurity. Either way, most children are astute enough to understand what is happening.

Far from fostering goodwill and liking for the step-parent, it may, in fact, be counterproductive. Although children can appear on the surface to accept the largesse on offer, they may actually be harbouring deep feelings of revulsion, despising what they see as adult hypocrisy. The lesson is, that we can't buy love. And we certainly can't buy respect.

What we can do—as parents and step-parents—is to make a genuine investment in the child's life. It has to be genuine because, as we've already observed, children can see through hypocrisy. It must also fulfil all the criteria of investment. It will be costly in terms of time, of effort, of self-interest. The first premium, and every subsequent premium, will include all those elements and more—sometimes in equal measure, sometimes not.

At times it will appear to demand all our resources, leaving us feeling drained and impoverished. But to give up is unthinkable; the surrender value is practically worthless.

No—if we're to reap dividends, it has to be an investment for life. Ruth and Steve are one of the couples who have seen their investment grow in leaps and bounds.

> *I play snooker with Kevin once a week, and Ruth spends time with Tracey. I remember Jack* [their church leader] *saying that there's got to be a time to stop commanding* [your children] *and to start communicating* [with them]. *I feel we've done that— going out regularly together and playing snooker. We've got a good relationship. We can talk about anything. I've even told him* [Kevin] *if he wanted to live with his mother anytime, he could. I wouldn't stand in his way.*

Ruth agrees:

> *He's a sensible boy and a reasonable boy. He might go through a teenage rebellion, but I don't think it would be because his parents have split up, but just because he's a teenager.*

Terry, having invested all that time and effort in mending bikes and building rabbit hutches, feels that he has as good a relationship with his stepdaughter as Steve has with his son.

> *She always felt she could talk to me about the divorce* [her parents'] *whereas she couldn't to Isobel because of upsetting her. In that sense, I suppose I was like an outsider.*

Meeting with surprise from Isobel, who said he had never told her, Terry responded:

> *That's how I felt it had to be. They [his stepdaughters] wanted a private conversation.*

Then on reflection he added:

> *If it was something important I'd have told you.*

John admits that his daughter tells Dawn more than she tells him. But whilst he appears to accept this with equanimity, his response, as Dawn points out, is not always conducive to harmonious living.

> *It makes it awkward for me [when her stepdaughter confides in her] because I don't like to keep things from John. Sometimes, if she's shared something with me and I tell him, he goes straight back to her to try and sort it out. I've told him I've got to be able to share things with him, without him taking it back to her, otherwise she won't trust me.*

It was obvious, from speaking with John, that he was motivated by a sincere desire to help smooth things over for Dawn. His sincerity, however, was obviously misplaced as far as she was concerned.

A better ploy for parents in this situation might be for them to be open with offspring. If a father or mother were to say to their child: 'I know there will be things you might find easier to talk out with... and I want you to know that that's okay with me,' then everyone would know where they stood. True, it would demand a certain level of trust on the one side, and loyalty on the other: a tacit acceptance that no member of the family would ever talk needlessly or maliciously behind any other member's back. But if that could be achieved, it would certainly have the effect of diffusing potentially harmful feelings of betrayal on all sides.

There would be no need for any guilt on the part of child or step-parent, nor for jealousy on the part of the natural parent. Each situation could be treated with the degree of confidentiality that it deserved and, most importantly, with which the recipient feels comfortable. The wise step-parent will never allow him/herself to be coerced into keeping secrets from the parent, if it will:

- be a burden to him/herself to do so

- in any way hurt the parent, or

- cause damage to the child.

It is often the case that because a step-parent is less deeply emotionally involved with the children than the natural parent, he/she is better equipped to see things more clearly. This ability to be objective can work to the benefit of all concerned—but only if the temptation to play God is resisted. If a situation arises in which the knowledge or involvement of the parent is paramount (say advice on, or help with, an abortion, a criminal offence or drugs) it behoves the step-parent to make it abundantly clear to the child that his/her parent has the right to be informed.

In this case, the step-parent might suggest that the child should relay the information him/herself. But we need also to make the child understand that they have our full support. And that we will, if they require it, put that support to practical use: accompanying them in telling both natural parents if asked; enlisting the help of the authorities where appropriate; and in any and every way possible—within our means.

Only through the patient exercise of love and trust will we come anywhere near reaping the dividends of love, affection, trust and loyalty—none of which may become apparent for years. Only then, will we have come anywhere near establishing something like a 'normal' family. Whatever that may be!

Part III

Ongoing Repairs and Maintenance

9

Mending Fences, Building Bridges

For all sorts of reasons—from underlying feelings of guilt, to society's prevailing attitudes (real or supposed)—those of us encountering problems in our stepfamily can often fail to recognize them for what they are. We may be quick to put the blame fairly and squarely on our circumstances. Or we may appear to defend our corner. We may even put up a façade of normality; but deep down we fear that we're about to prove the pundits right: stepfamilies *do* generate more problems than 'normal' families. And because of this entrenched belief, it can be easy to overlook the fact that at least some of our problems owe their existence to nothing more sinister than 'normal' family living.

Building strains

Conflict has been defined as 'a clash of wishes'. Since distance precludes a clash (or collision), it follows that this can only take place between people whose lives have become intertwined. And the more closely intertwined those relationships become, the more susceptible they will be to the strains of clashing wishes.

We see it all the time in 'normal' families: parents clash with teenagers and teenagers with parents. Husband clashes with wife, and mother clashes with father. Sometimes grandparent clashes with parent (over grandchild's upbringing) or in-law clashes with in-law (over anything). 'Clashes of wishes' cover numerous topics: drink; drink driving; money; curfew; personal hygiene; personal territory; responsibilities—to home, family, work; personality; sloth and slovenliness; mannerisms and mode of communication—I could go on *ad nauseam*.

It *is* 'normal' to have to face conflict in these areas. But unless we recognize the problems facing us as falling into the range of 'normality', those of us in stepfamilies may be in danger of chastising ourselves for having 'created' the problems. We blame our selfishness in wanting to remarry, the wrong choice of partner, or any one of a myriad reasons. But this sort of response is not constructive, and can actually trigger further areas of conflict.

Rather than trying to find someone to blame, it would be more helpful if we were to find solutions. For all of us 'going through the mill', there are guidelines to assist us in this area. Most of the problems encountered by parents, step-parents and stepchildren can be categorized in one of three ways:

■ natural strains—those that are simply a part of normal family life, such as personality; adolescence; pre-menstrual tension; menopause or redundancy

■ circumstantial strains—those that stem from insecurity, such as feelings of loss of people, possessions, privacy

■ disorientation strains—those that stem from confusion, such as split loyalties (see Chapter 10); a change in priorities (see Chapter 7); changing values.

Establishing which of these groups they fall into (there may be more than one) is crucial to understanding the nature of our problems. This has to be the first step if we are to find resolutions, because only then can we decide upon the most appropriate action.

Natural strains

Personality

In this respect, I am reminded of a letter I received from one of my closest friends, Stephanie, the wife of Canon Michael Cole, on the eve of my wedding to Paul:

> *...I want to send you all our love, and wish you every happiness for the future. It's a big step you're taking and if I try to put myself in your place, I imagine it has taken courage and faith. There will be the inevitable problems—but then which marriage is without those? Your temptation will be to think that it's you, because knowing your striving for perfection, you are a hard taskmaster for yourself! However, if there is one thing that Michael has taught me it's always to talk things out—and he's insisted on this even when I've been really obstinate! And the one thing that the Lord has taught me, is to be ready to say 'sorry' even when I'm quite convinced that it wasn't my fault. If you could be here, you would hear me laughing—Michael will tell you that it's never my fault—or so I say!*
>
> *Seriously though, I know that I can't pray—at least I can pray, but God can't hear me—if I haven't said sorry, so I'm on a losing wicket all the way round! I've just thought that I sound like an old Granny! Forgive me, I just long that you should be really happy and accept yourself!...and I'm sure that you're going to go on proving that 'God is able to keep that which I have committed unto him...'*

Stephanie was referring to my state of mind following the breakdown of my first marriage. I had become brain-washed into believing that the failure was all mine and, despite the counselling I had received, she was concerned that my natural perfectionism would persuade me that I—solely and personally—would be to blame for all problems encountered after my re-marriage.

Because of this (as yet unresolved) flaw in my personality, I took the precaution of viewing my judgement as unsound, and frequently sought the advice of a second trusted friend when it came to sorting out specific problems. Another vicar's wife and mother of a large family, like Stephanie, she was at least able to tell me what constituted 'normal' family behaviour. And to keep my perspective in balance until such times as I gained in confidence.

Adolescence

For Isobel the problems were different.

> Linda, my youngest, was stealing from the local shop. She felt the man in the shop was overcharging so she was getting their [sic] own back. She felt he'd stolen from her and that she was, therefore, in the right.
>
> She was completely unrepentant. Terry and I went down to the shop with her to discuss it. But I don't think we had control. She had. She felt she was right and that was all that mattered. We had to bring her father in eventually.'

Terry adds:

> It was me that phoned him. I felt he would carry more authority. Partly because of his being her father and partly because of his job [as a policeman].

It was clear, from talking to Isobel and Terry, that being part of a stepfamily had nothing to do with Linda's behaviour. She simply believed, with all the naive arrogance of a teenager, that she was in the right. The sort of thing that all parents of teenagers have to learn to contend with during those hair-tearing years!

The sort of thing that Dawn, too, had to endure—without recognizing it for what it was. She felt angry when John accused her of moaning about the way his children left their dirty dishes lying around for her to pick up.

I did more for his daughter than I did for my own.

Because his first wife had been a 'moaner', John couldn't cope with what he saw as similar behaviour in Dawn. Having had custody of his children since their mother's departure, he felt anyway that his daughter wasn't doing enough around the house. The fact that Dawn did everything for her—even her washing and ironing, which she'd not done for her own daughters—did not please him at all.

I told her she must put her foot down and not let her get away with anything.

But Dawn didn't find it that easy.

I felt sorry for her because of the years she had no mother around, and I wanted to make it up to her.

The trouble was, that despite her good intentions, Dawn often felt put upon, as she finally admitted.

I feel I must go gently, and not sort of boss her, because this is her home.

130

John's daughter was, in fact, manifesting perfectly normal adolescent behaviour; behaviour which had been in existence prior to Dawn's marriage to John. However, for reasons we shall see in a moment, Dawn had initially failed to recognize the signals. Had it been her own daughters who were leaving their dirty dishes all over the place she would not have hesitated in chastising them in the way of all responsible parents. She would have been anxious to instil into them the sort of self-discipline and thoughtfulness to others, that go into making our children the well-mannered, responsible adults of the future. It was because this was a step-daughter that she felt unable to make a 'normal' response.

Circumstantial disturbances:

Loss of self-esteem

John and Dawn were able to talk out their differences. They realized that Dawn's feelings towards John's daughter stemmed, partly, from a sense of her own insecurity. Because she was suffering from a sense of 'loss'—in that she no longer felt mistress of her own home since she'd moved into the house John had shared with his children since the departure of their mother— she dared not risk further loss. Disciplining John's daughter represented such a risk: the loss of her stepdaughter's esteem and, more importantly, perhaps the loss of John's support also.

Consequently, though commendable, her motives in wanting to 'make up' to her stepdaughter for the years she'd been deprived of a mother were simply pandering to every adolescent's dream: namely, to be able to sit back and be waited on hand and foot!

The insecurity that Dawn experienced is common to many parents and step-parents and, unless recognized, it can have the same adverse effect. So, too, is the feeling that there are two codes of practice in operation when it comes to the discipline meted out to children and stepchildren. More usually, however, that is the reverse of Dawn and John's situation.

In the way of all siblings, there will inevitably be complaints of unfairness—but, in the stepfamily, these may well be more justified than most. Inevitably, there will be times when the natural parent feels that the step-parent is prejudiced against their child, and when passions run high.

Each member of the family has to learn to accept that we can never satisfy 'all of the people, all of the time'. But whilst it is unrealistic to suppose that a step-parent can feel the same level of affection, or impartiality, for a stepchild, as for their own flesh and blood, we can take steps to minimize the damage.

Only by talking out our sense of frustration, of insecurity, of injustice—as calmly and as non-judgmentally as possible, as a family—can we ever hope to come anywhere near resolving the dilemma. This means accepting the limitations of our situation and asking for help with *my* feelings, rather than pointing the finger at anyone else.

Fortunately, John's daughter had already experienced the special brand of love that her stepmother brought to the family. Dawn's daughter, Amy, had sent her a birthday card. And because she'd been unable to find one in the 'Sister' category, she had written it on, herself. It was that generosity of spirit from Dawn and her family that eventually won the day.

Spoiling without rendering spoilt

For those of us facing similar situations, where good intentions may be obscuring clouded motives, the best solution to wanting to 'spoil' a deprived stepchild is to find more positive and less corruptible ways of doing so:

- baking a favourite cake or pudding occasionally

- doing something together—just the two of you: shopping, swimming, cinema

- buying his/her favourite magazine—and sharing an interest in the contents of it

- discussing the options and decorating his/her bedroom—together

- helping him/her to make him/herself a fancy waistcoat

- taking him/her fishing

- doing an evening class—together.

The difference between these things and the sort of 'spoiling' that Dawn had shown her stepdaughter is that most of them involve 'togetherness' and interaction. They are relationship-building. Consequently, they are unlikely to foster selfishness or thoughtlessness in a stepchild; or to leave a step-parent feeling 'put upon'.

Loss of parent and/or possessions

To be effective parents, we need to be able to differentiate between the sort of misbehaviour that is common to all children and adolescents, irrespective of family status—and that which is due to other causes. Like step-parents, stepchildren too, can be subject to a great sense of loss and insecurity. This may manifest itself in rudeness and anger.

I am reminded of a child who, when admonished by her stepfather to sit up at the table and not to slouch over her food, shrieked at him: 'You've no right to tell me what to do. You're not my real father.' And herein, perhaps, lies the root of the problem.

Gavin was on the receiving end of a similar experience. After his marriage to Carol he moved into her house whilst they awaited the sale of both his and hers, in order to buy a place between them. Watching the news on TV one evening, he was absolutely incensed when his young stepdaughter marched into the room and changed channels without so much as a 'by-your-leave'. A furious row ensued. 'Well, it's our telly, not his,' Natalie shouted tearfully when her mother intervened.

When she refused to apologize, she was sent to her room to cool off. Gavin, meanwhile, felt an 'absolute cad' for having reduced her to tears over 'something so trivial'. But as Natalie's mother, Carol knew that the problem ran deeper than trivia.

After a suitable period had elapsed, Carol went to great lengths to explain to her daughter that, with certain exceptions, marriage and family life entailed the sharing of possessions. And that although we should always respect the personal property of individual members of a family and never invade their right to privacy and sole ownership of some items, televisions came into the category of pooled assets. She reminded Natalie too that, although Gavin might not own the TV in the sense of having purchased it, the electricity which ran it and the licence which gave them the right to watch it were in his name and had been paid for out of his pocket. 'Only he doesn't rub our noses in it! And neither should we about whose TV it is,' she finished.

Carol and Gavin were fortunate. Natalie was a sensitive and thoughtful child, and her display of temper was out of character. Apart from minor incidents, which were clearly a result of her sense of loss and insecurity, there were no more major skirmishes. But for many children, it is an affront to their sensibilities to see a step-parent taking over what—to their mind—is essentially the role of a natural parent. Far from being placated by assurances that the step-parent now takes care of them by paying the bills or running the household, this may, in fact, only inflame their resentment.

Anger transferred

It is important to realize here the complexity of this type of resentment.

■ There may be deep anger against the absent parent who, in the child's eyes, has reneged on his/her responsibilities.

■ Paradoxically, there may also be a burning animosity against the natural parent for 'ousting' the absent parent.

■ Since proximity (in the second instance), plus an innate sense of loyalty, prevent the child from directing that anger at either natural parent, it finds its expression in other ways. It becomes articulated by means of transference.

The step-parent thus becomes the target for the child's ill-feeling. To the child's mind, this is quite valid. Stepmother or stepfather, in taking on the absent parent's responsibilities, is actually underlining that parent's abdication. It is as if they are rubbing the child's nose in it—and setting themselves up, in the process, as superior to the absent parent. If we suspect that this is the subconscious reasoning behind a stepchild's bad behaviour, then we need to take stock before taking action.

■ It is vital to the child's well-being that neither the natural parent, nor the step-parent sets about a character assassination of the absent parent. To hear an absent parent maligned can only add to the child's feelings of loss.

■ Instead, it might be appropriate to tell them that we will always attempt to answer their questions honestly and openly, but that there are some things which are beyond their ken at present.

■ In the meantime, we should do all that we can to reinforce in the mind of the child, the fact that his/her welfare is of paramount importance to both parent and step-parent alike.

Anger internalized

We saw earlier that rudeness or anger may be the outworking of a child's sense of loss—particularly the loss of a parent following bereavement or divorce. Sometimes, however, that anger may be internalized and emerge in another form. If a child lays the blame for the departure of a parent (through death or divorce) at his/her own door, that anger will reflect those feelings of culpability.

In this case, it may be self-destructive, as in the case of anorexia, bulimia, drugs or even, in extreme cases, the ultimate rejection: suicide. It may be attention-seeking, manipulative, or a cry for help. We see this in the children who suddenly turn to wanton vandalism, sexual permissiveness or criminal behaviour. Deep down they may be driven by an unrecognized rage to hurt the parents who hurt them. Alternatively, they may wish to force both estranged parents together in the common aim of resolving the mess in which they have landed themselves.

Two of the families we spoke with had major problems with children turning to drugs, and two others where children turned to shoplifting. My own daughter became a heroin addict following the break-up of my first marriage. Her reasons—stated years later—were precisely those given above: an initial desire to 'escape' from the unhappiness at home; a desire to punish us, her parents; and an overwhelming urge to reunite us in the common cause of her welfare.

Keeping a perspective on this sort of traumatic behaviour can be difficult when you've remarried. A guilt trip on the part of the natural parent is almost inevitable at this stage. But if the problems began long before remarriage (as ours did) then we need to remind ourselves of this. Without minimizing the problem or the child's trauma, we need to do whatever is necessary to maintain our own equilibrium. A calm, sensible approach is far more likely to produce constructive results than histrionic attempts to apportion blame. Besides, I personally, know of several stable, loving, two-parent families who have had to endure the trials of watching one of their children go through the throes of drug abuse, criminal activity, incest or abortion. Such things are not the prerogative of stepfamilies. Nor, necessarily, of bad parenting.

So what can we do in such circumstances? I was warned that it could destroy my second marriage if I allowed my daughter—who was living away from home at the time—to move in. Whilst I wanted to avoid that at all costs, I have to say that I could not have turned my back on her. To have had to do so would, I think, have put my marriage under more strain than taking her in proved to do. But had Paul not been the sort of man that he was, and had we not shared a strong faith in the goodness and power of God, I honestly don't know how we would have survived.

All I would say, in circumstances as extreme as this, is that the natural parent should guard against becoming manipulative. Pressure put upon a step-parent to take in a stepchild who has previously left home may backfire. It may be far better to treat the problem from a distance: seeing the child regularly, seeking all the counselling and help that can be mustered, and rallying a group of friends for emotional support, and prayer, if appropriate.

Letting go

As a last resort, however, there comes a time when we have to let go of a wayward child—even, perhaps, forcing them into taking responsibility for their own actions. This was the conclusion I reached with my daughter, after twelve years of trying to help her beat her addiction.

I realized that it was as if we, her family, were a cushion, shielding her from the worst effects of her drug abuse, yet helpless to shield her from the long-term, cumulative damage she was inflicting upon herself. And though it was the hardest decision I have ever made in my life, I saw that to go on 'helping' her was actually no help at all; that in continuing to take her in every time she hit a low, we were actually preventing her from 'hitting rock bottom': that place from which we have no place to go but up!

As a Christian, I already believed that when we are at 'rock bottom' Christ is there. Now I had to reach a new point of understanding. One whereby I could trust that, in denying Sally a bolt-hole whenever she was in trouble, I would not be abandoning her but would be committing her to the care of her heavenly Father. And like the parent in the story of the Prodigal Son, I had to expect the anguish of watching her go through the equivalent of 'eating pig-swill'. As I have said, it was the hardest and most painful conclusion I have ever had to arrive at.

It so happened that having reached a decision, I was able to stand firm in my conviction that this was the right thing to do. For Paul it was not so simple. As my husband he supported me wholeheartedly. As Sally's stepfather, however, he was full of ambivalence. Feelings of doubt vied with feelings of guilt. Tormenting oneself with questions like: 'Am I agreeing to this because I honestly believe it to be best for my stepchild, or because it would it make life easier for me?', it is natural for a step-parent to feel concerned, also, with what others will think of their motives.

At one time, when Sally was close to death's door, we wept together, our faith tested to its utmost. And though, ultimately, Sally came to her senses, we had to accept that there was no certainty about the matter.

Reaching this point is never easy. The road to this sort of commitment is strewn with the memory of failed good intentions. James Dobson's book *Love Must Be Tough*, and John White's *Parents In Pain* chart the agony of past failure, and the difficulties that lie ahead for parents caught in a dilemma of this nature. But confronting the problem also brings relief of a sort. As John and Dawn found.

For months they had to endure the heartache of John's son's stealing until, eventually, the boy moved out into lodgings. To begin with Dawn nursed a terrible guilt, convinced that she was responsible in some way. When John wept openly, her feelings intensified. Unable to vocalize their separate hurts to one another, the barriers went up. It was at this point, as we have seen, that her daughter Amy stepped in to heal the breach. She insisted that her mother and stepfather bring all the old misunderstandings out into the open. As Dawn confided later, it was the best thing that could have happened. It brought a new sense of commitment to their marriage.

Loss of perspective

So far we've defined the issue of bad behaviour as the manifestation of some deep-seated insecurity. But there are people whose malevolence is not so easily excusable; people who appear to have no motivation, yet whose perspective on life is so grossly distorted that their jealousy, like that of Colin's stepmother, can blight the life of a stepchild.

> *My father was a very generous man—always lending his tools to his neighbours, or giving away quantities of home-grown veg, or bunches of his prize chrysanths. My stepmother hated it. She used to complain that it cost her money. But it was even worse if Dad wanted to give me something. She'd follow us out to his tool shed so as to deny him the opportunity. It made him devious. If he wanted to slip me something—a tenner or a tool—he had to do it in an underhand sort of way that was embarrassing—to him and to me. Then she'd make an awful scene if she found out.*
>
> *It made me reluctant to accept anything from him. I felt I had to keep him at arm's length all the time.*

For a while after Colin married, his stepmother seemed to improve.

> *It was as if she saw me as less of a threat once I had a wife. But then when Dad wanted to make a gift to my wife, it all started up again. Even if he gave us a kiss goodbye she'd become petulant, wanting to know where her kiss was. I'm not sure who I felt most sorry for: her, my father, or myself.*

If Colin's solution was to distance himself from his father in order to give his stepmother no opportunity for reproach, his father's answer to the problem was quite the opposite. He spent his whole time trying to boost his wife's self-esteem with extravagant and very public displays of praise, pushing his son and daughter-in-law into doing likewise. Not only was it embarrassing all round; sadly, it was to no avail. As we have already seen from the way in which she altered her will, Colin's stepmother's jealousy and insecurity followed her to the grave and beyond.

Loss of confidence

Not all jealousy and insecurity take quite such an extreme form—nor are such feelings the prerogative of step-parents. The natural parent, too, can show signs of acute vulnerability. However, when the root cause can be ascertained there is much more likelihood of its being resolved. Pam, for instance, was quick to see that her reaction to Chris's old badminton partner was due to residual insecurity from her first marriage.

> *Soon after we were married, I took a telephone call from a woman asking for Chris. When I learned later that she was ringing to see if he would start playing in matches again— and that he'd agreed—I saw red.*

The thing was we'd moved to Chris's town where he'd lived all his life and I knew no one. I just saw the whole of my first marriage repeating itself—when I'd been the little 'house-mouse' stuck at home with the children and my 'ex' had been living it up with a variety of Other Women.

Pam hit the roof. She shouted, she railed and she sobbed. The strength of her reaction left Chris dumbfounded. And the more inarticulate he became, the more Pam's passions were inflamed.

I wanted him to deny that there was anything for me to get worked up about, but I knew if he did that I'd just shout him down because that was what my 'ex' used to do. I felt so horribly vulnerable. It was as if I was right back in all the morass of hurt from my first marriage...

Once I calmed down, of course, and we talked it out I began to see reason—and Chris was able to understand my feelings. The situation was quite different. He wasn't anything like my 'ex'.

Pam's feelings amounted to a temporary loss of confidence, occasioned by something that had happened in her past in conjunction with her current situation. It was quite different from the usual sort of insecurity because she recognized it instantly for what it was. Although ferocious in its intensity, it was short-lived and probably owed its existence to nothing more sinister than the natural upheaval caused by her move.

Disorientation

Confusion; changing values

For some people, this loss of confidence can take a more extreme form, amounting to a loss of faith in the whole ethic of remarriage. 'I feel as if God is punishing me,' wept one woman when everything appeared to be going wrong between herself and her husband.

Another divorcee, who for seven years had delayed marriage to the man she loved, found that when they eventually married she was quite unable to sustain the relationship. Although outwardly citing all the faults as his, it was clear from speaking with her that she was riddled with guilt and self-condemnation. Subconsciously, she believed that this second marriage was against God's will.

This is not an issue for everyone. And even for those for whom it is, doubts of this sort may be transitory and fleeting, triggered by nothing more than fatigue, or perhaps a careless remark at a time when we are already feeling 'snowed under'. But for some, this sort of dilemma can be a serious, and potentially damning conviction: the certainty that they had no right to be remarried in the first place.

Such scruples owe much of their existence to misunderstanding. Small wonder, when so much of the Bible and Christian thinking on this subject appears to be conflicting, that some people, at some time or another, are plagued with niggling uncertainties about their position. We are all human; all subject to the frailties of our emotions and our intellectual comprehension. The Christian viewpoint is that we are, also, all targets of the devil—the Father of Lies—whose mission is always to undermine our trust in God, the Father of Love. For them—and also for those to whom the promises made in a church wedding are less a matter of Christian faith and more an issue of moral integrity—is there any reassurance to be found? Or is there nothing for it but to have to live with the belief that we've made a mistake?

It is true, according to the Bible, that divorce can never be God's ideal will. In the Old Testament book of Malachi he is stated as saying: 'I hate divorce.'[19] However, nowhere does he forbid it. On the contrary, because of the hardness of men's hearts in divorcing their wives for no good reason, provision was made in Moses time (to which Christ later referred) to safeguard the welfare of such women. Divorce, though lamentable, is, therefore, broadly speaking, an accepted part of the Christian tradition.

Much of the confusion since then seems to stem from the mistaken idea that whilst this may be so, remarriage is total anathema. Yet as Guy Duty points out in his book Divorce And Remarriage, Old Testament law dissolved a marriage in such a way as to allow a woman to 'go and be another man's wife.' 'When the woman married the second time,' he writes, 'she did not have two husbands because God spoke of the first as her *former* husband.'[20]

It is also true that Christ, himself, spoke of adultery in connection with remarriage—but to accept this prima facie is to take it totally out of context. What is being said here is that if a man divorces a woman on a mere whim, then he is the cause of his second marriage being 'unlawful' in the sight of God. Such a statement takes for granted the woman's right to remarry following divorce.

Guy Duty stresses that remarriage after divorce is not the issue. The case rests on whether the divorce is permissible or not in the first place. If it is, then the right to remarry is automatic. According to New Testament teaching, divorce (and therefore remarriage) are permissible for Christians in the following instances:

■ where marital unfaithfulness has already broken the 'one flesh' relationship of marriage [21]

■ desertion by a non-Christian—in which case the believer is 'not bound'[22]

■ where divorce has occurred prior to someone becoming a Christian, remarriage may subsequently take place on the grounds that the new Christian is 'a new creation' and that 'the old has passed away'[23].

And this, really, is the crux of the matter for anyone who continues to feel guilty, or to believe that God is punishing them for having made a second marriage. First of all, because no matter what the rights or wrongs of the situation, Christian belief rests on a just and loving Heavenly Father, not a vengeful God who is arbitrarily punitive. If we admit our wrongdoing and want to start again, God is 'faithful and just and will forgive us our sins and purify us from all unrighteousness.'[24]

In this way, no matter what the wrongdoing, we may be forgiven and made 'a new creation'—every day. The Bible states that there is no condemnation for those who follow Christ;[25] that it is for freedom that he has set his followers free, and that they are to stand firm and not allow themselves to be 'burdened again by a yoke of slavery'.[26]

That 'yoke of slavery' may be self-imposed; or it may be implied by doctrinal ambivalence in different denominations. From the Church of England (whose policy is not to conduct a wedding service but to 'bless' a second marriage conducted elsewhere)—to those Baptist Churches which will, under certain circumstances, remarry divorcees but, by their own constitution, deny them any office or leadership—confusion reigns. Such uncertainties do little to give the peace of God to those seeking guidance—whereas a little unconditional love goes a long way, as these contrasting experiences show:

'I felt second-class for a good twelve months with the church,' said Terry, voicing the feelings of several Christians who were divorced or had married a divorcee.

'It was the total acceptance that got to me,' said Steve, moved by the quality of love he'd found in his church.

10

Exits & Entrances: Access

All the world's a stage, And all the men and women merely players; They have their exits and their entrances

As You Like It by William Shakespeare

Access is usually arranged by the courts at the time of divorce, in order to give estranged parents certain rights that enable them to continue a relationship with their children. These may include an order for visitations:

■ weekly—which may only be of short duration, say a few hours at a time

■ for the whole or part of a weekend—to be spent in the residence of the estranged parent

■ for school holidays—to be apportioned between both parents

■ and for Christmases—to be either alternated or divided between the two homes.

Traditionally, access is vested with visions of wet soggy days spent tramping the streets in search of shelter and some form of entertainment, whilst struggling to maintain some semblance of normality between parents and children who have suddenly become strangers to one another. The film *Kramer v Kramer* portrayed, in tear-jerking fashion, the agonies and insecurities of this sort of situation, where both parents and child are caught on the twin horns of emotion and litigation. The evidence showed conclusively that no one can win. And the message was that the terms of access can never, at *all* times, meet *all* the aspirations of *everyone* concerned.

The stress-factors of access

The family in the film was relatively straightforward, comprising mother, father and small son. But the more multi-faceted the structure of a stepfamily—in other words, the more personalities there are involved—the greater the potential for conflict arising out of access.

Access is a two-way business for many stepfamilies. There are the incoming children who visit us—those who live with their other parent, who also may or may not have remarried and have stepchildren. And there are the outgoing children—those who live with us, but visit their absent parent's new family.

This can be yet more complex. We may find ourselves, as a step-parent, living with the children of our spouse, whilst our own live with our ex-partner. Alternatively, it may be our own offspring who reside with us, and our stepchildren who are the visitors. Then again, none or all of the children of each of us may reside at home.

A further dimension is added—as the infamous Woody Allen/Mia Farrow affair served to remind us—with adoption of Third World children and others of ethnic minorities more commonplace these days. One woman relates her experience.

Because Kylie was black she already had problems of identification. She was only a baby when she was adopted, so she grew up thinking 'white', and spoke of her own kind as 'them', whilst we were 'us'.

When I got divorced she suffered a terrible sense of rejection. My other two girls—my natural daughters—were grown-up enough to make their own arrangements to see their father, whereas Kylie was still quite young. She found it all very difficult when he didn't make much effort to see her.

Then when she became a teenager and wanted to start dating she discovered that not everyone thought of her the same way as she did about herself. She felt a misfit; neither black nor white. It was as if she was rejected all over again.

For different reasons, this sense of rejection echoes thousands of others. One of the saddest aspects of divorce to my mind, is when children and the parent who does not have custody of them become estranged. Causes may be numerous:

■ the departing parent may simply disappear and renege on all responsibilities

■ he or she may decide upon a 'clean break' settlement in order to set up home with someone else

■ the custodial parent may make access so difficult that the absent parent has no recourse but to go back to court

■ conflict between both parents over access may reach such a pitch that the absent parent becomes convinced that it would be kinder to the children to sever all ties

■ geographical and economic restrictions may make access a virtual impossibility

■ or perhaps it is simply a question of access rights going by default.

The frequency factor

Most 'experts' are of the opinion that access with the absent parent is crucial to a child's welfare. Opinion amongst parents is not so clear-cut. And where each estranged parent has remarried, children themselves can find their loyalties stretched to the limit. For instance, there are those who would like to see their absent parent more frequently:

Their father has access whenever he wants, but it's never as often as the children want. He only rings when it suits.

Invariably, it's when they contact him. If they waited for him, he wouldn't contact them at all.

It was hard knowing Dad was Dad to her children and doing things with them when we hardly saw him.

Sometimes, infrequency of access is due to lack of thought or sensitivity on the part of the absent parent. Several stepfamilies felt that last-minute requests to see the children made no allowance for the fact that *they* had a life to lead.

To begin with Dad hardly saw us at all. We would have liked to see more of him but he was always too busy. A year or two later, when we'd all settled into a routine, he'd ring wanting to see us there and then and be put out when we didn't want to break arrangements we'd already made to see friends.

He'll say: 'you can come this weekend' and then Claire will say: 'I've got a disco.'

Often this leads to resentment on the part of the absent parent, the custodial parent, the step-parent, and the children themselves. The child resents being made to feel guilty—torn between previous arrangements and contact with the absent parent—who in turn may actually believe that difficulties are being raised arbitrarily and wilfully. If those suspicions are correct and the custodial parent does have a hidden agenda whereby access is being deliberately blocked, a core of ill-feeling will result, which is potentially explosive.

The secret of success, in situations like this, lies first of all in open communication; the sort that leads to an understanding of the feelings of all concerned. And secondly in attitudes that are both flexible and tolerant. Something like: 'I realize it's difficult for you to make long-term arrangements, and Johnny really wants to see you, but we're already committed to going away. How about we keep next weekend clear, and you see if you could manage something then?' will go much further towards improving relationships all round than: 'You're always the same! Expect everyone to drop everything for your convenience. Well, it's not on, and that's it!'

A little give and take on both sides works in everyone's favour, as Ruth and Steve discovered.

> *We try to be flexible with Steve's second wife seeing Kevin and Tracey.*

> *She's no problem anyway. She never married the father of the twins she had before she and I got married, so she understands the problems from the other side. I brought the twins up as mine when we did marry, and we used to restrict their father's access for my benefit. So she realizes that Ruth needs to know where she stands with Kevin and Tracey. Yvonne's like a favourite aunt to them. But all their maternal needs are met in Ruth.*

This family, despite all its convolutions, succeeded in achieving amicable arrangements all round. This was due to a mutual tolerance and flexibility, whereby each was able to appreciate the other's point of view.

As step-parents, as custodial parents, and as absent parents, we need to ask ourselves hard questions. How often do we foster ill-feeling in our children, in ourselves, in our partner and ex-partner by: our lack of understanding; of tolerance; of standing in the other parent's shoes; of making allowances for genuine difficulties? A few honest answers might make a world of difference to our stress-levels all round.

The insecurity factor

Where there is good reason to believe that the custodial parent is being deliberately difficult in raising objections to access, we need to ask ourselves: Why? Why should the parent of any child persistently deny them access to the other parent when all the evidence indicates that to do so is detrimental to their wholeness and happiness? We may find that there is more than one answer. Perhaps the most obvious is the state of mind of the parent with whom the child lives, as Peter recalls:.

> *There was a definite resentment on the part of my ex-wife when I had the children whilst I was courting Sandra. She was afraid I would take them to visit her. It was obvious that she said things to the girls to put them off.*

Having been in the position of being an ex-wife and single parent myself, I confess that, whilst I would not condone attempts to influence the children adversely, I have *some* sympathy with those sentiments. Divorce is a traumatic business and leaves no one unscathed. A good deal of rejection and insecurity attaches itself to the 'abandoned party'—especially if the departing spouse already has another partner. Insecurity breeds fear. Fear of further hurt, loss and rejection. Fear that the child might be wooed away by the other parent—or find that the step-parent has more to offer than we have ourselves.

Unfortunately, such insecurity is not the prerogative of the abandoned parent—who at least, more often than not, has care and control of the child. It finds its breeding ground also in the mind of the absent parent, to whom each date for access carries with it the anxiety of wondering whether the event will measure up to the child's expectations. And where there is a third party involved—a 'friend' or step-parent—fear multiplies.

It is in the nature of fear to manifest itself in one of three ways: Freeze, Flight or Fight. It's easy to see how these present themselves between warring parents.

■ Freeze
There are those who believe that if they do nothing the problem will go away—the so-called 'easy option'. This may account for access rights not being taken up by the absent parent—not because access is seen as undesirable, but simply because the moment of confrontation is put off for so long that ultimately it appears well-nigh impossible to reinstate it.

■ Flight
Parents who take flight actually make a reasoned decision to curtail access to their child. This may be motivated by selfishness, as in the parent whose self-interest convinces him/her that it is not worth the effort to maintain contact. Or it may be the result of a (mistaken?) belief that it would be better for the child if all ties were severed.

■ Fight
The Fight mode may not always be as obvious as taking the matter to court. A more insidious form of fight is

achieved through propaganda: out-and-out brainwashing of the child; more subtle forms of parental character assassination; or simply a 'drip-feed'—offering alternatives to the child that are designed to diminish the merit of anything the other parent can offer.

There are monumental emotional forces at play in divorces and remarriages that involve children on either side. Feelings of insecurity are present all round, from the child who fears that the departure and remarriage of either parent spells an end to parental love and the custodial parent, who is terrified of losing the child's affection to the parent who has right of access, to the absent parent (usually a father) who feels his back is already against the wall, and the poor old step-parent who feels like piggy in the middle. Nonetheless, whichever position we find ourselves in, for everyone's sake it behoves us to be as objective and dispassionate as possible, and to endeavour to do all we can to ensure that:

■ we're at least charitable to one another—how would we feel in the other's shoes?

■ before jumping to conclusions, we make some effort to understand the reasons behind the problems of access

■ we realize that if the happiness of our children is our main concern (as it should be) then we need to be big enough to set aside any pettiness arising from our own hurts

■ we desist from 'scoring points'—whenever humanly possible! (I found silent recitation of the Lord's Prayer a help during 'difficult' phone calls)

■ and that we create the sort of atmosphere in which our children can flourish.

If we are the parent raising objections to access—either overtly or covertly—then we need to be scrupulously honest with ourselves about the nature of those objections. Sounding out our arguments with a trusted friend is as good a method as any other to ensure impartiality. It would be churlish to stand between our children and their other parent merely on the grounds of our own insecurity. And if this is our only motivation for denying access, or making it difficult, then we need to do all that is humanly possible to overcome our shortcomings.

It's a tall order—I realize that—and it's doomed to failure from time to time. But the stakes are high: our second marriage, our children's happiness, our own self-respect, and enduring relationships all round. In my book, it's worth keeping those things in the forefront of our minds. For if we fail in this respect, we risk having our children, and our spouse, turn on us in the future, denouncing us for our selfishness!

The common-sense factor

There may, however, be other related circumstances for denying access. For instance, it would be quite right, in my opinion, to protect children from exposure to a string of 'live-in-lovers', or persons of dubious character, or simply untenable situations. One woman discovered, on an occasion when her daughters were visiting their father, that they had been left alone in the house whilst he and the woman with whom he was living went out. As one of the children was asthmatic, naturally the mother was extremely concerned.

Another mother, believing her children to be spending the weekend at boarding school, was alerted by staff at the school that her ex-husband had arrived with his mistress to take them away. This sort of conduct is insupportable. Not only did it put the school staff in an invidious position, it could also have caused the mother untold suffering had the children's absence not come to light until after the event. Additionally, it spelled out an unacceptable level of behaviour to the children and, in doing so, demeaned their father in their eyes.

Naturally, the mother put a stop to all impromptu access of this sort, by taking it up with the school, the children's father and the children themselves. Until it was pointed out to them, they had simply not thought through the ramifications.

These situations are extreme and demand extreme intervention. On the other side of the fence are those parents who express concern, for example, about their children being taken to the pub; or about perceiving a lifestyle which is the antithesis of what they want for them. They have a point. But having said that, we can hardly expect our ex-spouse to exist in a vacuum! There are bound to be 'Mummy's boyfriends' and 'Daddy's girlfriends'. If those relationships are to have any chance of success, then inevitably they will eventually have to involve our offspring.

We may be tempted to dismiss any consideration for our ex-partner's new relationships as nothing to do with us, but such attitudes are short-sighted. They are deserving of our concern, if not for the sake of decency, then for the sake of our offspring. As has already been pointed out in earlier chapters, it is not fair to our children suddenly to spring a new step-parent upon them. Children need time and opportunity to adapt to the new situation, to develop a relationship with their absent parent and, where appropriate, to form a new relationship with the potential step-parent. But more than that, they need the freedom of knowing that we release them to do so. Free of guilt.

We have to be realistic. And in the aftermath of divorce this can be extremely difficult. The heart is deceitful above all things, and it is the easiest thing in the world to rationalize; to convince ourselves that we have 'just cause' in preventing our children having contact with their absent parent's new 'friend'; to persuade ourselves that we are acting in their own best interests.

This may be far from the truth—and it may take a trusted friend or counsellor to tell us so. Someone who can show us, without causing offence or further hurt, that if our motivation is, in fact, a deep-seated vengeance for the hurt we have sustained, then it is nothing more than spite and self-indulgence. And since manipulative, self-justifying spite is learned by osmosis, then if this is the example we are setting our children we should know that it is a highly unattractive trait we're passing on. In a very real sense, we shall be 'spoiling' our children.

What's more, we risk damaging their mental health and emotional stability, and may, in the long run, ruin their own chance of happiness. At very least, we impair their sense of security.

The manipulation factor

Manipulative behaviour can take more subtle forms. Chief among them are the financial inequalities that may exist between parents and step-parents. Costly gifts, extravagant forms of entertainment, holidays or simple cash payments on the part of one parent may be seen by the other as attempts to 'buy' a child's affection.

That may or may not be a conscious intention—it matters little to the more impoverished parent, who feels distinctly disadvantaged. Step-parents who have taken on their spouse's children are in an equally invidious position; Ruth, for instance. Steve was vaguely aware of resentment in her whenever Kevin and Tracey spent time with their mother, but he was unable to put his finger on the reason until Ruth explained.

> *Tracey used to boast with her friends when they were saying: 'I've got this, or that.' 'I've got two mums!' she'd say. That really got at me. She'd even tell strangers.*
>
> *I tried to talk naturally about Yvonne so Kevin didn't feel he had to choose sides, but I found it difficult when she gave them sweets and so on. But then I realized that in her position I'd be just the same...*

Where only one parent has remarried, feelings of inadequacy may be redoubled. To the single parent struggling on alone on a diminished income and with no one around to give any moral support, the sight of a child returning laden with gifts from a weekend spent with the new stepfamily is enough to send all but the hardiest into a paroxysm of contempt (for the absent parent), self-pity and despondency.

I recall weeping on the telephone with a friend when my girls returned from the first weekend they spent with their father. Boats on the river at Henley, lunch at pubs frequented by TV stars and lavish gifts which included huge boxes of chocolates were as nothing compared to the fact that they had been to the theatre. Armed with T-shirts of the show, catalogues of the show, and long-playing records of the show's hit music, they regaled me with details of the seats they had occupied—in a private box. My middle daughter openly admitted that she had spent more time watching people watching her lording it up than she had watching the show.

It was hard not to feel jealous. Harder still not to feel ashamed. And downright impossible not to feel frightened. Frightened that they would find life with me too dull. Frightened that they would prefer to be with their father.

My friend assured me, as a mother herself, that children know which side their bread is buttered and that ultimately, once the excitement had worn off, the security of home would prove more enthralling than boxes in theatres. I'm not so sure that this is always the case, but I'm happy to report that it was for me. And that my ex-husband was ultimately sensible enough to desist from this sort of competitiveness.

It's hard to be objective when you're in the midst of a situation like this. But the fact is that, if we could only distance ourselves from the distress of our feelings, we would see that, more often than not, the absent parent is feeling just as vulnerable as we are ourselves. They know the truth of what my friend had to tell me, that no matter how often they play the Wizard of Oz and Father Christmas wrapped up together, they are up against something far more abiding: the security and stability of twenty-four hour parenting.

The jealousy factor

'Daddy won't love you any more now he's married her,' one mother told her daughter.

'You'll be at the back of the queue,' said another when the girl expressed a wish to go and live with her father and his new family.

Loyalty to the parent with whom they live may force children to an intellectual acceptance of this sort of statement, whilst their emotions are telling them something quite different. Pulled in two directions, they may end up isolated and alone, turning in upon themselves because of their inability to cope with the insidious pressure put upon them. For their own sakes, as well as a genuine desire to be 'fair', I made it a point of honour never to run down my ex-husband (or his wife) to my girls, nor to allow them to do so without good reason.

No less difficult to deal with, however, is the step-parent who slanders the natural parent, remembered here by one stepdaughter, now adult:

> Though I'd love to see him alone, I still can't stand going to stay with my father, or even meeting him for a meal, because Sylvia always comes. She never lets me have any time on my own with my father. But she spends her whole time running down my mother and my sister. It's as if she thinks that just because I've left home I don't get on with my family. She does it in a conspiratorial sort of way, putting her arm through mine... I think she thinks it will please me. As if we're allies— she and I against my mother.

If the aim of the step-parent is to establish some sort of rapport, this is hardly the best way to go about it. Nor will it foster good relations between child and absent parent, because the implication is that the latter is the source of the slander.

It appeared that this young woman's father lacked the moral fibre to stand up to his second wife for fear of being thought to defend his first wife. How much better it would have been if he'd been able to point out to her the damage that she was inflicting. The father might have told his second wife that although he privately agreed with all she had to say about his first wife (which would have had the effect of allaying her insecurities) it would be preferable not to involve his daughter. And if that failed to curtail the gossip, he might have pointed out that it could prove counterproductive—as was the case with another young woman and her stepmother.

> *She quite literally cannot stand the sight of me now. Even to my face she makes snide remarks, though she's careful never to be too hostile in front of my father. But nothing is sacred. My figure, my hairstyle, clothes, boyfriends, job—and of course, most of all my mother.*

When jealousy becomes as vociferous as this, the only course of action may be for the child or adolescent to tell an adult, and ask that access be restricted to the absent parent only. And if the natural parent is too timid to stand up to his spouse, then so be it. It certainly isn't the child's place to have to do battle with a step-parent.

The split-loyalties factor

Even where relationships are good within the stepfamily, it is as well to expect that there will be a some sort of kickback from children in the aftermath of access with their absent parent. However well adjusted they may appear to be at home, contact with estranged members of the family—parents and siblings—is bound to present them with a conflict of loyalties. A confusion of emotions is inevitable.

Hannah is a case in point. She was fourteen at the time of her mother's remarriage, but from the outset she and her stepfather, Alan, built up a good relationship together. They shared a similar sense of humour, a mutual pleasure in sport, and were both quiet, methodical people.

To begin with, Hannah's father hardly availed himself of the 'reasonable access' granted him by the Courts. If Hannah felt hurt, she hid it well. But there was always a subdued sense of excitement about her whenever she was presented with the opportunity of seeing him. The trouble was that each time she returned from a day out with her father and sisters (both of whom were living away from home) the tension and antagonism that emanated from her was tangible. She took it out on Alan, picking on him for the least little thing, criticizing everything about him and causing unprovoked rows between the whole family.

Easily moved to tears, she became increasingly insecure. She began to imagine that her mother favoured Alan more highly than she did her. 'You've given him more mashed potato than me,' she'd accuse her mother, petulantly and unreasonably. Yet within days, she would settle down again and assume her usual diffidence, interspersed with moments of sparky good humour. Alan and Val were quick to realize the cause.

'It's just a question of split loyalties,' said Alan, generously dismissing the often hurtful behaviour of his stepdaughter.

He advised Val to tell Hannah that he was not in competition with her father for her affection. Before doing so, Val had a word with her eldest daughter, Mary.

Mary said that Hannah probably felt guilty because she got on so well with Alan. She thought that Hannah probably expected to have the same easy-going relationship with her father, and when it didn't work out like that because they'd become strangers to one another, it made her feel even worse. We decided that she took it out on Alan because she saw him as the cause of her feeling so bad.

Val was able to take Hannah on one side and ask her whether she felt that, if she showed affection for Alan, there wouldn't be enough left for her father. To begin with Hannah wasn't sure. But when Val explained that love is not like a cake which you cut into slices, she began to understand.

> *With cake, the more people there are wanting a slice, the smaller the slices become. And when you've cut the whole cake up and distributed it and then someone else comes along, there's nothing left over but crumbs.*
>
> *But love is the opposite. It isn't diminished by the number of people on the receiving end of it. It actually grows. The more people there are to share it out to, the more it expands.*

Val reminded Hannah of a song she had sung in primary school, pointing out the merits of love when you give it away: 'Love is something if you give it away, you keep on getting more.' Then she pointed out that Hannah's father and stepfather were two entirely different people, and that it was perfectly possible to enjoy a different relationship with each, without fear that the one would detract from the other. Within a short time, the matter was resolved.

Steve's son, Kevin, had similar problems with split loyalties. He was only five when his father and Ruth married and he barely remembered his mother's presence full-time. Nevertheless, he obviously enjoyed seeing her whenever he and Tracey went to visit. His dilemma came when he was brought home.

'He wouldn't say goodbye to her,' said Ruth. 'Dear little chap! It was as if he was trying to shield his father.'

As parents and step-parents, we need to be aware of our children's sensitivity to our feelings. It would be easy to embarrass or bruise them by drawing the wrong sort of attention to their actions—poking fun at them, or censoring them for their 'churlishness'.

The best way to ease their unease is for us to endeavour to talk as naturally and amicably as possible with our estranged partner. Perhaps we could reach some sort of agreement whereby we undertake never to discuss our differences in the presence of our children. But if that proves impossible, then it may be a better option for the step-parent to take on the responsibility of handing over and receiving children from their other parent. This was Isobel and Terry's solution.

Isobel never has any contact with her 'ex', because there's always been conflict between the two.

It arose over school fees. In front of the children he said he wouldn't pay for my younger daughter.

The constant friction made Isobel ill. Eventually, Terry told the children's father that in future all arrangements—for school fees, holidays and so on—were to be done through him. The proposal met with approval all round and has proved successful ever since.

Ruth, too, has succeeded in being mediator—not only between Steve and his previous two wives, but between the women themselves. Inevitably there have been times when both ex-wives have met on the doorstep, but Ruth has handled it well. Steve believes that God has helped Ruth with any resentment she felt at the beginning with Yvonne—and it is certainly true to say that there is harmony between the two. Gratifyingly, Yvonne chooses to confide in her. And whenever she rings to make enquiries about her two children, Steve makes a point of passing her over to Ruth, saying it's her department.

When it comes to his first wife, he is generous enough to acknowledge that she has done a good job in bringing up their two girls, but he has his regrets.

*It's been fourteen years since I lived with them as a father.
The eldest still comes round, even though she's eighteen, but
she's been a bit difficult at times. I think their mother talked
about me in front of them.*

However, Steve doesn't feel that his first wife has
consciously turned his daughters against him. He thinks
that although she is happy to take the praise when all is
going well, when it goes wrong, she blames him. He, on
the other hand, sees the failure of her second marriage,
and the fact that she has had a number of boyfriends as
a contributory factor in the girls' problems.

*It suited her not to have me around. She never consulted me.
I love them all equally, but it tears my heart out knowing I've
not been there to tuck them in, share all their fears and
foibles. And there's been no one to replace me.*

At one point the eldest accused her mother of being a
failure. But Ruth and Steve are clearly of the opinion
that it would be detrimental to encourage the children
to be disloyal.

'She won't run her mum down in front of us,' said
Ruth. 'Both girls are very supportive towards her. The
eldest mothers her mother.'

With six children and three homes to be considered,
Steve acknowledges that access has to be flexible. He and
Ruth try to have all the children under one roof one weekend in four. He feels that the more there are the easier it is.
However, if it happens that Yvonne wants the middle two,
he and Ruth accept this quite philosophically, and see it as
positive in that it gives them more time with the older two.

*They all get on well—enjoy the same sports. We take them out
for a meal quite often. Sometimes I take them without Ruth so
they've just got their Dad.*

Ruth agrees that this is important. Steve feels that there are 'no visible scars' and that everything is as 'perfect as it can be', but he admits that he only sees the good side.

Peter and Sandra fared less well when they were newly married, experiencing split loyalties between the children of both sides: Sandra's, whom she had custody of, and Peter's, who lived with his ex-wife.

> *My kids, at one time, resented enormously that I was with Sandra's children seven days a week and with them only one. There was this very natural resentment when Sandra's three gave me a kiss. I suppose it makes me over-compensate with my three. I felt I had to overcome this enormous hurt I'd inflicted on them.*

Sandra's and Peter's solution was to discipline themselves in the way they reacted to both sets of children, and to point out to each other the areas in which each overreacted. They also went to great lengths to see that Sandra's children, who were 'in residence', so to speak, were more sensitive to Peter's when they came to stay— as she explains.

> *Sometimes we pray with my girls and point out how Peter's kids feel when they come down. The girls [hers] know what it feels like from when they visit their father who has a stepdaughter. They restrain themselves from seeking affection when Peter's kids are down. They hold back.*

Through their joint efforts they have achieved much in the way of creating harmony when Peter's children visit them. However, Peter admits that he has been unable to talk out the issues with his own children. Part of the problem is that, because he was not a Christian when married to his ex-wife, he feels that her attitudes to his new-found faith inhibit him.

Despite attempts on the part of Peter's ex-wife to put the children off visiting, it was obvious that the girls were torn between loyalty to their mother and a strong desire to see not only their father, but also Sandra's girls.

We'd arrange to spend the weekend separately, and Peter's girls would keep asking him: 'Aren't we going to see Sandra's girls?' It just didn't tie up with what their mum was saying.

They became increasingly confused about what they wanted to do, and with whom they wanted to be doing it. One weekend, when arrangements had been made for them to sleep overnight at Peter's and Sandra's house, the youngest asked to be taken back early on the Sunday morning in order that she might go to a party. It meant Peter would then have to take the other two children back later. Aware of his tendency to over-compensate, Peter held his ground.

We said to her: 'You have to choose. If you want to see us, come; if not, don't.'

He and Sandra made the girls realize that if they had something else on, they were free to choose not to come, and that whatever their choice, it would not adversely affect their relationships. The youngest daughter, however, remained undecided. Having agreed to visit Peter for the weekend, she then arranged for her stepfather to collect her in time for the party.

For sometime thereafter, she would ask what her father's plans were, weigh them up against the other possibilities open to her, and make her decision on the basis of what Peter called: 'hedging both ends towards the middle'. Needless to say, it taxed every ounce of his and Sandra's patience to deal with her.

The legal factor

There are important differences in English law between a Custody Order and a Care and Control Order which are not always fully understood. In simple terms, Care and Control is to do with the ordinary day-to-day responsibility for the welfare of the children who reside with us. This covers feeding, clothing, housing, schooling and so on, but would not extend to the larger issues such as sending a child to boarding school, or giving a minor permission to set up home alone, to get married or change religion. These decisions are the prerogative of the parent who holds the Custody Order.

In some instances, custody is given to one parent and care and control to the other. This means that all major decisions would have to be referred. More usually, custody is given to the parent with care and control, or alternatively, jointly between parents.

Legally, neither parent may take the child out of the country for any length of time without the permission of the other or, *in extremis*, that of the courts. This is intended to protect the absent parent's rights of access. Obviously each case has to be looked at individually and if it could be proved that emigration was in the child's best interests (if, say, the mother married an Australian sheep farmer) then this would be taken into consideration. Whilst this may be a rarity, one other factor is more commonplace.

We have already looked at the question of how children should address a step-parent, and the isolation that this can cause if they find that they are the only one calling them by Christian name, rather than Mum or Dad. What we have not considered, is the child's feelings of discomfort at being known by a different surname to the rest of the family. Remarriage does not confer any rights in this respect.

Some children feel distinctly insecure being known by a different name to their mother, and whilst this is more likely to affect the young, teenagers, too, may feel embarrassed. Isobel's children were given permission by their natural father to take on Terry's name—but as Isobel discovered, that was not the end of the matter.

> *They wanted to identify with Terry and me. So whenever they had to bring letters home they were addressed in my new married name. But although they had their father's permission to use his surname, they certainly didn't have their grandmother's!*

Isobel's daughters were known by Terry's name throughout primary and junior school, but when it came to the time for them to go to secondary school, their paternal grandmother made it clear that she refused to pay the fees unless the girls reverted to their father's name. Isobel felt she had no choice but to comply; and happily, because the girls were now older, they had no problem in adapting.

Under duress, Sandra's ex-husband agreed to his daughters taking on Peter's surname, but Peter's own children elected not to change to their mother's new name. This might have something to do with gender. Given the choice, maturity, and intellectual capability of making a decision, boys are less likely to opt for a change in surname than girls. Quite possibly this is due to the fact that girls often relinquish their surname on marriage, whilst a boy is expected to carry on the family name.

There is a danger that in exerting pressure upon children and their non-custodial parent to permit a change of name, we may be doing so for the wrong reasons. A second marriage severs, as nothing else can do, the 'one flesh' of the first marriage. The temptation then can be to cut off the past completely in the hopes of creating a new family unit with no divisive history behind it. That, sad to say, is a forlorn hope. It is also, quite probably, a selfish one. In any question of a change of names, the only real consideration is that the feelings of the children should be paramount.

11

Extensions: the Wider Family

Certain events warrant special mention: Christmas, coming of age parties, weddings, and so on, because they force step-parents and parents to look again at the implications of membership of the wider family. Many, for whom the question is hypothetical as yet, prefer not to think too deeply about such issues. Others make plans to exclude the absent parent from certain functions, only to find that in the event, the saying: blood is thicker than water, is not only an old one, but a true one.

Marrying the old with the new

Val, for instance, had never encouraged Mary in her determination not to have her father walk her up the aisle, but privately she could understand her reasons.

> *It just seems hypocritical to me. He hasn't been a father to me while I was growing up, because he hasn't lived with us. Frankly, I think it would be more appropriate for my grandfather—or even my stepfather—to give me away. They've both been more of a father to me.*

When it actually came to it, however, Mary found she was unable to stick to her principles.

I just couldn't do it. It seemed too much like a slap in the face for him. And whatever he had done to us, I couldn't do it back to him.

She approached her mother with a certain amount of trepidation, only to discover that Val was in full agreement with her change of heart. Nonetheless, Mary still felt strongly that to have her father 'give her away' would be totally inappropriate. She spoke to her minister who assured her that, even though she would be walking up the aisle on her father's arm, it would be quite in order for the words: 'Who giveth this woman to be married to this man?' to be omitted from the service. In all other respects he was accorded a father's place.

Another woman, Betty, who had been a single parent for over twenty years, had to face a similar situation when her only son got married.

When my son asked his dad [to the wedding] I thought: 'What's he ever done for him?' He walked out when Andy was only a toddler. Then I discovered that Andy had been seeing him on and off for some time, without ever letting on to me. It was like a knife in my back.

Even when the decision has been made to include the absent parent, the problems are not over. In fact it's more than likely that they are only just beginning! When Kate was to be married, she and her fiancé had clear ideas as to what they wanted: all the men officiating were to be in grey morning suits; the wedding breakfast was to be a sit-down meal; and she wanted her father to be on the top table as well as her stepfather—but was adamant that her father's wife (with whom no love was lost) should be seated elsewhere.

Her mother, with whom she lived, reached an agreement with her father to split the costs. The trouble was that his second wife then felt that this gave her carte blanche to have a say in all the arrangements. There was opposition to the colour of the morning suits, the venue, the guest list and—of course—the reception itself. Kate's mother was at her wits' end, and confided in Kate's stepfather,.

> It seems to me that when you're divorced, you're left to bring up your child on your own—without any interest from her father until there's a stepfather to take responsibility—then you fly around making all the arrangements for the wedding reception (which you want to do because you love your daughter); you do battle with your 'ex's' wife when she wants to take over; then as the bride's mother, you have to take a back seat whilst the bride's father waltzes in and takes all the limelight!

Kate's stepfather offered to take a back seat too if that would help to appease her father's wife, but Kate and her fiancé stuck out for what they wanted. However, though the wedding went off with great style and enjoyment, there were underlying currents of tension and discontent which might—with a little more understanding and selflessness—have been avoided.

Matured materials: coming of age

It is not always the step-parent who is the cause of dissension, however, as Dawn's experience shows.

> I did an eighteenth birthday party for John's daughter. It wasn't how we would have done it; it was exactly as she

173

> *wanted it. I did all the catering, but I spent a lot of my own*
> *money making it nice for her. But John's mother told me*
> *afterwards that his ex-wife had said how mean we were.*

The remark was particular cruel and cutting because, although Dawn admits that the affection she feels for her stepdaughter is not the same as for her own daughters, she has always gone out of her way to treat them all the same. What's more, her stepdaughter knew that. Which is probably why the remark was made in the first place!

> *She wanted to open her presents early—before the day—but I*
> *wouldn't let her. I wanted it to be a special day for her. I said*
> *to her: 'I do for you what I do for my own daughters,' and*
> *she said: 'Well, I am your daughter now, aren't I?'*

Displacement: illness and funerals

Illness and funerals are other occasions which can cause consternation amongst members of a stepfamily. When an aged aunt from our ex-husband's side of the family falls terminally ill, for example, should we be expected to brush aside the many years of affection and companionship we have shared with her? I think not. Nor should we feel excluded from a funeral. We can't cut ourselves off from genuine feelings of mourning, simply because a divorce has cut us off from our spouse.

Nevertheless, it calls for a certain level of self-confidence to carry off making an appearance alone at an event at which you are bound to encounter your ex-spouse's new partner—especially if you are unsure as to your reception from other members of the family or your place amongst the mourners. My ex-husband and I have always maintained a relationship which is civil enough to allow for eventualities such as this. Even so, I have usually found it more comfortable to accompany one of my daughters when visiting a sick member of their father's family, or attending a funeral.

There are occasions, however, that thrust you together in such a manner that the only way forward is to put the past firmly behind you. The death of my middle daughter last summer was just such an event. After twelve years of heroin addiction, followed by five years drug-free, it was particularly distressing to learn that she had died of asphyxia following an overdose of morphine, and that two people had been arrested in connection with her death.

The details are not relevant here. My reason for raising the subject is simply to point out that it would have been all too easy for my ex-husband and me to have thrown off all restraint and self-discipline, and allowed our grief to explode in an orgy of recrimination. Recrimination which, I am convinced, would have been as destructive for our other two daughters as for us—and as futile in doing anything to bring back our dead daughter.

Don't misunderstand me. We are not saints. There were moments that came dangerously close to just that scenario. But my ex-husband and I succeeded in talking, and in communicating our compassion for each other in our loss in such a way that we were able to agree to work together harmoniously and with dignity, for the sake of all concerned.

It meant that *my* second husband and *his* second wife had to take a back seat at times. But though I can only speak for Paul, I know that this was done with a generous heart and with a real desire to do whatever was necessary to support us all, as a family. I believe that we achieved our aims. What's more, the tragedy of losing our daughter has brought home as nothing else could, that divorce and remarriage can never totally sever the ties of parenthood that bind a couple together.

Continuity in building: adding on

In this respect, one of the happy events of remarriage must surely be an addition to the family. Though it may be a shock to some and a financial struggle to others, a new baby is seen by most couples to be a confirmation of their love for one another; a cohesive factor in the stepfamily, linking the siblings of each partner uniquely, genetically and irrevocably with one another.

Nonetheless, step-parents planning to extend the family need to think very carefully before launching into parenthood. For some, the question is, anyway, purely academic. Isobel, for example, had to have a hyster-ectomy prior to remarriage with Terry:

> *I have conflicting views on this. I'm glad for the girls' sake that I can't have babies but that's unfair on Terry—though he knew before he married me.*

> *That was the hardest decision, because I wanted children. My parents have two girls, so the family name dies.*

For those who have made the decision, it is simply a question of how best to tell the existing children that there is to be a new addition to the family. This will obviously vary according to age and gender.

> *I bought a book and showed Tracey what was happening when I was pregnant. She was four, but we really shared through the pictures. She really could understand.*
>
> *Kevin [eight] took it all in his stride... 'So what! No big deal...! What's for tea?'*
>
> *But it was a good opportunity to teach him the facts of life. He was interested. He'd get the book down...*

Reaction to the concept and actuality of a new baby brother or sister will vary from family to family. Steve—with three families—recalls:

Every time I've had another child, the eldest feels pushed further back.

Isobel's daughters are also ambivalent on the subject:

The girls openly admit to being more secure because they're the only ones on the scene. Their father's wife hadn't been married before. Her auntie is always pushing them to have a family and the girls feel very threatened by the thought that there could be another baby. It's come up a couple of times. We actually had to ring and ask so we could know how to handle it because they were in such a state. The second time it came up, Granny (their father's mother) told them not to be so selfish.

Ruth's stepdaughter experiences normal sibling tension:

Tracey feels put out now because she isn't the baby any more. When she goes to see Yvonne she's got her older sister who spoils her and she's the baby. When she comes home, she's the older sister, and she always reacts for a while. But she's back to normal the next day.

Steve admits that bringing up a third family late in life is not all plain sailing. Nevertheless, he considers it worthwhile.

Kevin's very good. He's a good boy. He helps us bringing up the two little ones. He lets us sleep in and he'll even change nappies. It was the broken nights I found difficult. But I'm a better father now than when I was younger.

... the pressures...! With six kids to support and babies waking you up at nights. I see colleagues with small mortgages, teenage children, all settled, playing golf... I sometimes feel under a lot of pressure...

But I wouldn't swap with any of those people that I envy when I'm tired. I love those little babies. I appreciate what I've got so much more. I really enjoy pottering around with them.

Frank's daughters were teenagers when he and Lynn married, and the prospect of two baby sisters simply brought out all their maternal instincts and did nothing to dent their self-confidence. Both older girls lived with their mother, but Lynn is sure that the babies have acted as a magnet on them and actually had the effect of increasing their visits to see their father and herself.

Tim was not so fortunate. When he married for the first time, his wife already had a daughter of three, whom he adopted legally. When his wife became pregnant again, the elder child became increasingly disturbed, playing up all night—even before the birth of her half-brother.

Tim might have convinced himself that this was simply the manifestation of the normal insecurity of a toddler anticipating 'displacement' by a new baby, were it not for the fact that things went from bad to worse. Now adult, the girl has been an unmarried teenage mother twice over, each time pregnant by a different man. He admits freely, that all was not as it should have been during the child's upbringing, that there were differentials made between her and his other children—though not on his part, he is quick to add. His mother (the girl's adoptive grandmother) never accepted the child, he says, and she refuses to this day to acknowledge that she is now a great-grandmother. Sadly, her attitudes are to her loss, as much as to those of the mother and child.

Grandparents: the golden gate

As the whole concept of what constitutes a family becomes ever more complex, so the boundaries become more obscure and, in some senses, more limiting. Grandparents were once a vital part of the family: the voice of reason and wisdom; a link between the generations; capable, willing and ever-ready to step into the breach of any crisis. To the uninitiated, it might be supposed that stepfamilies gain in this respect: that remarriage brings in its train all the cousins, aunties, uncles, and grandparents from both sides, and forges them together into some big happy dynasty. Sadly, the reverse is just as likely to be the case.

As little as one remarriage on each side is enough to produce as many as twelve grandparents: two pairs from each parent's first marriage, plus two from each of their second marriages. That potentially triples the number of Christmas and birthday presents grandchildren can expect to receive, and offers the couple a greatly extended choice of babysitters. Unfortunately, it also trebles the 'in-law' troubles, and increases the burden of 'duty visits'.

Any gain assumes an ongoing, harmonicus relationship with the grandparents of a first marriage, whether that marriage came to an end through divorce or death. In the first instance, there is more likely to be a degree of animosity; in the second, other factors may be at work.

When my middle daughter died six months ago, she left a toddler of twenty months. Naturally enough, in the midst of our grief, we were all concerned for the welfare of our grandson. Sally had not been married, but she had registered the baby in his father's name. Because they had not been living together for the last six months of her life and we were not sure whether Colin would cope with so young a child—or, indeed, that he would want to—Paul and I discussed the very real possibility of our bringing him up.

In many ways the prospect appealed. In other respects it was daunting. The thought of coping with teenage traumas when we would be drawing close to pensionable age was quite frightening, but we wanted to do the best by everyone concerned.

As it happened, Colin was only too happy to bring up his son. He is proving a very caring and responsible young dad, and is considerate and amenable when it comes to keeping us in touch with our grandson. Although they live at some distance from us, we see him whenever we are able, receive the occasional letter and photograph, and hope that we may have him to stay with us as he grows up.

I am aware that we have been fortunate. Under current legislation grandparents have rights of access. However, if those rights are withheld for any reason, the onus would be upon the grandparents to prove that they had been wilfully denied. Where there is considerable distance between the two families, that might turn out to be difficult, if not downright impossible—and in the meantime, *tempus fugit*.

One elderly couple discovered how easy it was to lose touch with the next generation. Devastated at the loss of their son from a brain tumour, they were doubly distressed when their daughter-in-law remarried two years later and, in order to establish a new life, moved a considerable distance from them. They felt in effect, that they had lost their grandchildren too. The probability is that those children will grow up knowing only their maternal grandparents and the parents of their stepfather.

That is only one side of the story, however. Some-times, as we've seen from Tim's experience in his first marriage, grandparents find it difficult to make room in their affections for stepgrandchildren. Maggie was another case in point.

> *We had major problems with my mother. She felt her grandchildren had their nose pushed out by Bob's children. I think she hates them. She had planned that I could go out to work after my divorce so that she could have my kids. So she hates Bob even more, because by marrying me he prevented that happening.*

Frequently, grandparents find it difficult to accept a new son or daughter-in-law. In Bob and Maggie's situation, things were further complicated by the fact that their marriage was only brought about because the ex-partners of each had run off together and ultimately married. That meant that they shared the same in-laws. Bob explained:

> *Maggie's mother-in-law, who was very close to Maggie during her first marriage, doesn't get on with my ex-wife, who is now her daughter-in-law.*

Maggie added:

> *The whole relationship between herself and Jayne has just deteriorated. She felt she had to come down secretly to see her grandchildren who, of course, live with us.*

Ruth and Steve know what it feels like to be in a similar position.

> *Steve used to take me over to his mother's. But it took a long time before we got on.*

She thought a lot of my first wife. They still see a lot of each other. I don't think that deep down my mother has ever really forgiven me for leaving her.

Terry fared even worse at the hands of Isobel's mother-in-law, as Isobel explained.

We've had our problems with the girls' grandparents. It's a matriarchal family and my mother-in-law poisoned the children's minds against their father after the divorce. But once Terry and I married, the scene changed. She made up with her son and made conditions about seeing them [the girls]. She was obviously afraid of not seeing them any more, but she began saying to them that Terry wasn't their father and that he shouldn't be in their house.

The relationship deteriorated and solicitors' letters followed, with unreasonable demands for access for the children's father—demands which Isobel's mother-in-law was instrumental in making. Eventually Isobel and Terry offered to vacate their home for two hours each week to make it available for Isobel's ex-husband to see the girls on their own territory. However, on the strength of a social worker's assessment, the girls' father backed down. The terms of access then agreed were less favourable than they were previously. Isobel is fairly philosophical about the ongoing relationship the children have with their father, his wife and her parents.

I know they go to see their stepmother's parents and have presents from them, but they never show them to me. They call their stepmother 'Auntie', and her parents by their Christian names.

Dawn and John's situation, through tactful and strategic handling at the outset, was a good deal happier.

My parents accepted John's children as part of the family. But although his mother kept saying how happy she was that we were getting married—so she wouldn't have to keep coming over to cook and clean for them—when it happened, she didn't want to let go. I felt awful about pushing her out, but I knew it wouldn't work if she kept coming over.

My brother forewarned me of possible friction. We had to be very tactful. She was expecting to come over as usual, so the first night back from honeymoon, I went to see her and asked her over for dinner on the Wednesday—several days later. That way she knew she wasn't expected before that.

John's mother took the hint. And although there was a certain amount of tension between the two women to begin with, ultimately they have succeeded in hitting it off reasonably well. But then Dawn has always seen the relationships in her stepfamily as opportunities for personal growth, and a chance to reach out to others in a caring way.

12

Doors and Windows

It has long been the practice of Christians to speak of life's choices and opportunities as 'doors' to be 'pushed' to see if they 'open'. In recent times, that sort of jargon has become more universal, only now—perhaps with the advent of 'computer-speak'—we talk of 'windows of opportunity'. Doors and windows, however, also have their more usual connotation, allowing us security within our homes; access to the world outside our homes; extending our vistas beyond our own four walls; shedding light on the events happening inside. I like to think that this combination of opportunity, security, access, outward vision and inner discernment is a picture of the 'ideal home'; something for us, as stepfamilies, to attain to.

I have spoken at length, throughout this book, of the problems that can beset stepfamilies, but my objective in doing so has not been to magnify those difficulties, nor to confirm any sense of hopelessness about second marriages. On the contrary. My aim has been solely concerned with the recognition that life is—by and large—a series of problems, and that in overcoming them, we develop the sort of character and perseverance that lead us to personal fulfilment of our potential—and with it the satisfaction of achieving a sense of purpose.

Windows of opportunity

Two of the couples who have shared their stories with us have found 'windows of opportunity' opening up for them in the most profound and life-changing ways. Their experiences may not be pertinent to everyone reading this book, but they are, nonetheless, worth a mention. First is Maggie, who for five long years struggled to cope with a stepdaughter whose adolescent traumas might well have wrecked her second marriage, to Bob.

> *By the time my stepdaughter was thirteen, I felt I was on the brink of a nervous breakdown... I didn't believe in the existence of God but eventually I said: 'If you're real, you'll have to show me.' And he did!*

Maggie, her second husband, three of their five children—and subsequently (through one of her daughters) her former husband—all came to know God as a direct result of the problems they encountered as a stepfamily. Their faith also helped them to cope, as a family, with the potentially self-destructive tendencies of her stepson, and helped them, ultimately, to help him pull himself around.

A door of hope

Steve and Ruth have a similar story of how God changed their lives. 'An inner emptiness' was how Steve described the driving force that compelled him to seek to fill it by whatever means possible. A shrewd businessman and charismatic personality, his search had led him through numerous philosophies, cults and sects, plus two failed marriages (each producing two children). After all the trauma (his second wife had left him with their two little ones to look after) Steve had been close to suffering a nervous breakdown. By the time he'd set up home with his girlfriend Ruth, who had moved in as 'surrogate mother', he was in a bad way again.

> Ruth was so lovely—not just to look at—she was everything a bloke would want in a wife. I wanted desperately to love her, but I couldn't. Something was dead inside me.

Because of that 'deadness' and his resulting inability to respond in a caring and loving manner to Ruth over the following year or so, the relationship looked doomed to follow the previous two. But God had other plans for Steve and for Ruth. As a last-resort attempt to save the ailing relationship, they had 'the holiday of a lifetime': a trip to America to visit Steve's sister. The experience was to prove a turning point.

> It was stepping out of the ordinary—seeing myself 3,000 miles from home. I cracked. I begged her not to leave. It all flooded out—all the hurt and rejection.
>
> My sister had a lovely family—and that broke me. There I was on tranquillizers and I thought I was going to die. I thought God was going to punish me.

Steve's sister was a Jehovah's Witness, but Steve had already explored the cult's doctrine and decided it was not for him. With the barriers down, he decided to have a look at Christianity and, as a result, had a really dramatic encounter with God.

Steve's conversion presented problems of a different sort, however. Whilst he was extremely concerned that the children should not lose Ruth—the only mother they had known for the past two years—he felt, as a believer, that he could no longer continue a sexual relationship with her. Ruth agreed to stay on to look after the children, but she was determined not to get involved with all the 'church and Jesus business'. Frankly, she found Steve's behaviour bizarre

> *I couldn't understand what he was on about. Actually, I felt quite hurt and rejected. Steve just didn't seem to want me any more.*

It was seeing the change in Steve, however, that eventually persuaded Ruth to look for answers for herself. Her ultimate conversion, her marriage to Steve, and the two children they subsequently produced, are all signs of the way in which God has worked in their lives. Now—more than twelve years later—they are still happily married; Steve's business prospers; and both are engaged in part-time Christian work. Moreover, as a direct result of Ruth's care and concern, she has succeeded in bringing about a reconciliation between Steve's first and second wives and has smoothed the way to better relationships between all six children.

Housewarming: heartwarming

The beautiful stories of what must surely be two of the most successful stepfamilies ever recorded can also serve as reminders of God's help. The first, from the Old Testament, tells the story of Ruth who, when widowed, refused to abandon her mother-in-law, Naomi—because she loved her 'better than seven sons'. Ruth's second marriage, to a relative of her dead husband, produced an heir—making a stepgrandmother of Naomi, of whom it was said that the child would 'renew' her life and 'sustain' her in her old age. It is clear, from the way that 'Naomi took him, laid him in her lap and cared for him', that this was a real Happy Ever After ending!

The second instance of a successful stepfamily is that of Mary, Joseph and Jesus. Supposing Mary to have had an illicit sexual affair during his betrothal to her (much more binding than our present-day engagement) and the baby she was expecting to be illegitimate, Joseph was intent upon breaking off their impending nuptials as discreetly and compassionately as possible. He obviously hadn't bargained for what was about to be asked of him! Urged by an angel—so we are told in the Bible's account—Joseph was finally persuaded of Mary's virginity and agreed to take on the child as if he were his own son.

That's a tall order, to be asked to step-parent the Son of God! But by all accounts one that met with success. Although it is recorded that certain tensions existed from time to time regarding Jesus' duty to his mother and stepfather versus his heavenly Father[28] and that the carpenter's son's 'street-cred' was not always all that it should have been amongst those who knew him most intimately,[29] it is clear, also, that the family enjoyed close and loving relationships.

We're told that Joseph shared his wife's anxiety following Jesus' disappearance after the Feast of the Passover, and Jesus' compliance and obedience to his mother and stepfather is mentioned as a consequence. Jesus evidently also followed Joseph into the family business. In addition, it is obvious that at least one member of the family, James, admired and revered Jesus enough to become one of the leading lights in the early Christian church.

Theirs was clearly a stepfamily worth emulating. An example to us all as to how to achieve that Happy Ever After ending.

References

1	Hebrews 11:1
2	Matthew 11:28, 29
3	1 Corinthians 7:8, 9
4	2 Timothy 1:7
5	1 John 4:18
6	Matthew 18:22
7	Matthew 7:26
8	Matthew 7:24, 25
9	Proverbs 24:3
10	Luke 14:28–30
11	The Koran
12	Exodus 21:7–10
13	1 Timothy 5:8
14	Proverbs 31:10–31
15	Deuteronomy 21:15–17
16	Proverbs 22:6
17	Proverbs 13:24
18	Ephesians 6:4
19	Malachi 2:16
20	Deuteronomy 24:3, 4
21	Matthew 5:32
22	1 Corinthians 7:15
23	2 Corinthians 5:16
24	1 John 1:9
25	Romans 8:1
26	Galatians 5:1
27	Luke 2:41–52
28	Mark 3:31–35
29	Matthew 13:54–58

Index

INDEX